THE PAUL TEMPLE

ROAD ATLAS for GARDENERS

of Surrey, W. Middlesex, S.W. London & West Sussex

FIND OUT WHERE YOU CAN:

- visit plant nurseries, garden centres & gardens open to the public
- talk to expert plant growers and buy your plants directly from them
- gather new ideas & products from plant centres
- gain inspiration from gardens open to the public
- pick your own fruit and vegetable

FEATURES:

- the plants in which each nursery specialises
- up-to-date opening days and hours
- information for the disabled
- and lots, lots more...

Road Atlas for Gardeners

The Paul Temple ROAD ATLAS for GARDENERS

© Beverly Cutress & Wimpey Knott 1995
All rights reserved.
The contents of this book, and the compilation and selection of entries included in it, are protected by copyright. No part of this publication or its compilation may be reproduced or transmitted in any form or medium or by any means, electronic, mechanical, photocopying, recording or otherwise, or stored in any retrieval system of any nature without the written permission of the copyright owners.
It may not be used as a basis for selling direct mail services to others. No part of this book may be used for compiling another list, map or directory. Information may not be copied from this copyright work and sent out for confirmation and correction.
Warning: the doing of an unauthorised act in relation to a copyright work may result in both a civil claim for damages and criminal prosecution.

The maps in this atlas are based upon the 1989 Ordnance Survey 1:50,000 scale Landranger maps with the permission of the Controller of Her Majesty's Stationery Office.
© Crown Copyright
They have been redrawn to the same scale and simplified to be easily read by motorists.
The scale of $1\frac{1}{4}$ **inches to the mile** (2 cm to 1 km) is much larger than that of conventional road atlases to make route finding easy.
The authors are building up a library of these large-scale road maps throughout the country. They are available on disk to interested parties by arrangement with, and written permission of, the publishers and the Controller of Her Majesty's Stationery Office.

Cover based on original design by Kate Bowen.

ISBN 0 948965 58 4

Road Atlas for Gardeners

How the atlas works

The roads shown in green on the maps highlight the easiest routes to the entries from the nearest 'A' roads.

Each entry is clearly identified with its own unique black lozenge number.

map page 38 ⟶ **38/4** ⟵ entry number 4

The map and text entries are always shown alongside each other on the same double page so that the location and description of each place can be seen without the need to turn the page.

All the places are marked on the maps but some entries are more extensive than others, in accordance with the wishes of the proprietors. Entries in the text have to be limited because they must face the maps. Those people who want to tell you more about themselves have therefore taken additional space at the back of the atlas in the section 'Additional Information'.

Occasionally you will find an entry which gives only the name. It is probably part of a large, well known group that needs no further description.

Access and facilities for disabled people and wheelchairs

We have endeavoured to include relevant information and hope that it is adequate and accurate. We would welcome any comments.

Changes and Mistakes

The opening dates, times and admission charges have been quoted to us by the people concerned. However, smaller nurseries can be a little flexible with their opening hours: if the ground is snow-covered or too wet to work, for example, they may decide to 'shut up shop early' or close for a well-earned, brief, winter holiday. In summer, some may remain open much later ...

> Therefore we cannot recommend strongly enough that you should telephone first if you are travelling from a distance or making a special journey.

We have done our best to ensure that all information in this Road Atlas is correct. However, as we deal with thousands of details in both entries and maps, it is possible that errors have slipped in. Please let us know of any slip you notice. As every reasonable care has been taken in the preparation of this book, we can accept no responsibility for errors, omissions, or damage, however caused.

Published by **The Factory Shop Guide** in collaboration with
Beverly Cutress & Wimpey Knott who have personally researched and compiled this book.
1 Rosebery Mews, Rosebery Road, London, SW2 4DQ
Phone: 0181 – 678 0593   Fax: 0181 – 674 1594

INTRODUCTION

Planning a gardener's day out in Surrey, W. Middlesex, S.W. London and West Sussex?

The Road Atlas for Gardeners will show you precisely where to go!

This book is a new idea!

It features specially drawn large scale road maps together with information about all the interesting places in the area open to gardeners.

It is the only atlas of its kind which leads you precisely to each place, showing the exact location and the most direct way to get there, whether from motorway or nearest town.

Gardens open to the public

We show the gardens that are open either throughout the year or on a substantial number of days so that you have a good chance of finding them open when you plan your day out. Current charges and opening times are included in the text. Many kind people open their gardens to the public on a few days each year for charity. They are marvellous to visit but they are well described in other publications and we thought it would be confusing to include them in this atlas. Please note that we have not included the entry charges to great houses, but only to their gardens.

Nurseries

Nurseries grow all or most of their own plants on the premises and sell them directly to the public – often at very reasonable prices. Other plants may be bought in to complement their home grown stock. Some specialise, others grow everything! All offer expert advice.

Opening hours can be flexible – many close at dusk in winter but remain open late in spring and early summer.

Some of the nurseries have international reputations and have won prestigious medals. Other nurseries are very small and supply their local community.

Please note that we have not included small specialist nurseries open only by appointment as these are described in other publications.

Garden Centres

Garden centres sell a full range of plants, shrubs and trees – some home grown, others grown-on and yet others bought-in. They also sell many other things for the gardener.

Small garden centres often carry an amazingly wide range of stock on small sites. You will usually meet the owners who are friendly, helpful and knowledgeable about their plants. They serve local gardeners well.

Medium sized garden centres are able to carry a much wider range of stock – more varieties of plants, shrubs, trees and, for example, gifts, books and bulky items such as garden furniture, paving and sheds.

Large garden centres are becoming more like department stores every day. Restaurants, aviaries, pet centres, swimming pools and conservatories are becoming the norm in addition to huge numbers of plants.

Pick-Your-Own Farms

The fields are only open when the fruit and vegetables are in season but wet weather can cause their temporary closure. Some pick-your-own farms also have farm shops. These are generally open throughout the year and sell a range of fruit and vegetables as well as their own crops. A few also sell locally produced speciality foods for the gourmet.

Names alone can be misleading!

- Gardens do not always include 'garden' in their names!
- Gardens often grow and sell plants!
- Nurseries sometimes include 'garden' in their names!
- Nurseries should sometimes be called garden centres!
- Garden centres sometimes grow most of their own stock, sell little else and could well be called nurseries!
- Garden centres sometimes sell few plants but many pots, paving stones and sheds!
- Garden centres should sometimes be called 'leisure centres' – they sell christmas decorations, children's toys, anoraks and many things unconnected with gardening!

As we said, names can be misleading!

So please use this atlas to explore and make your own interesting and worthwhile discoveries.

Every one of the places featured here has been visited personally by the authors but there must be others we have missed. If so, we hope they will forgive us and let us know so that we may include them in the next edition.

MAP PAGES

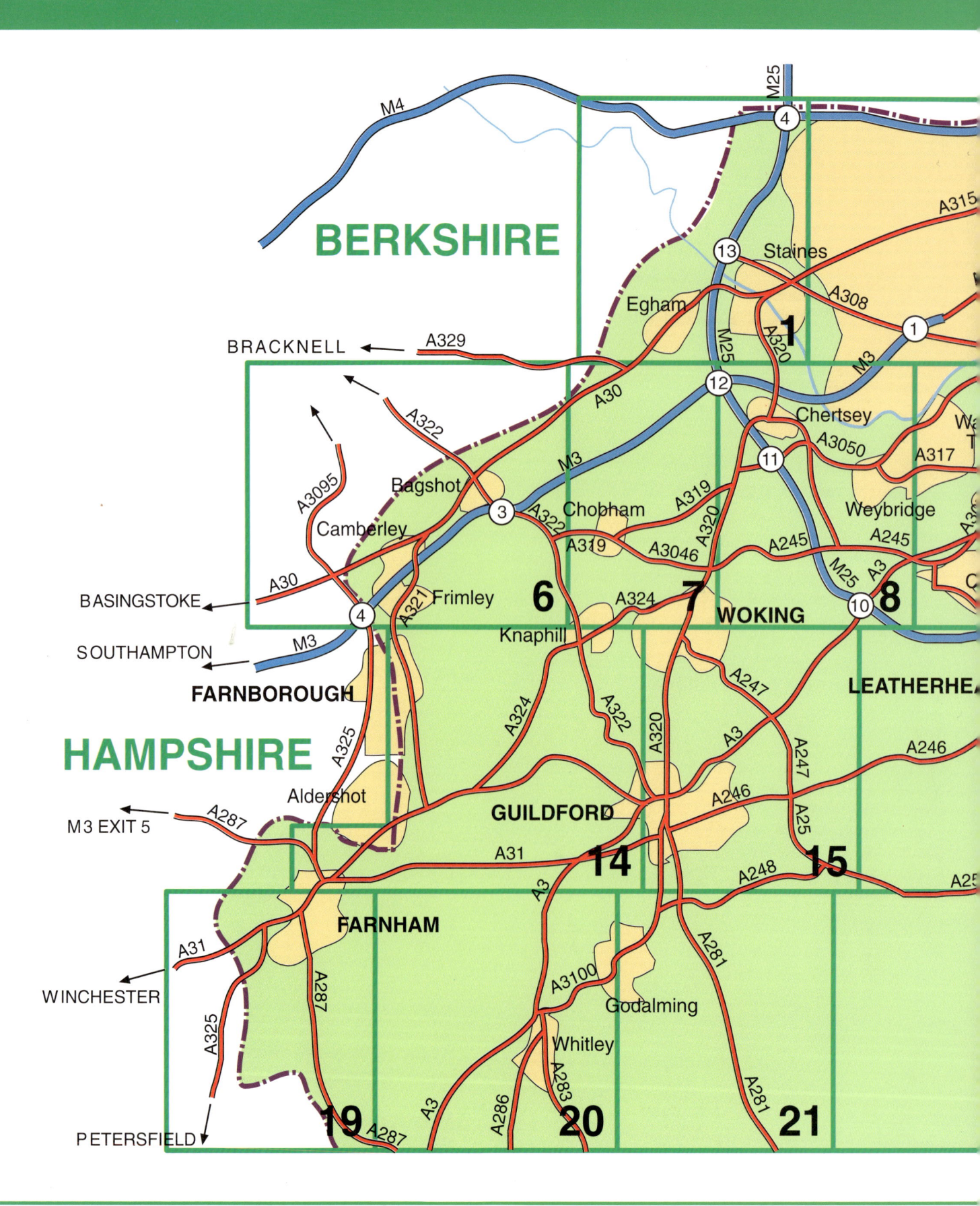

Road Atlas for Gardeners

SURREY, W. MIDDLESEX & S.W. LONDON

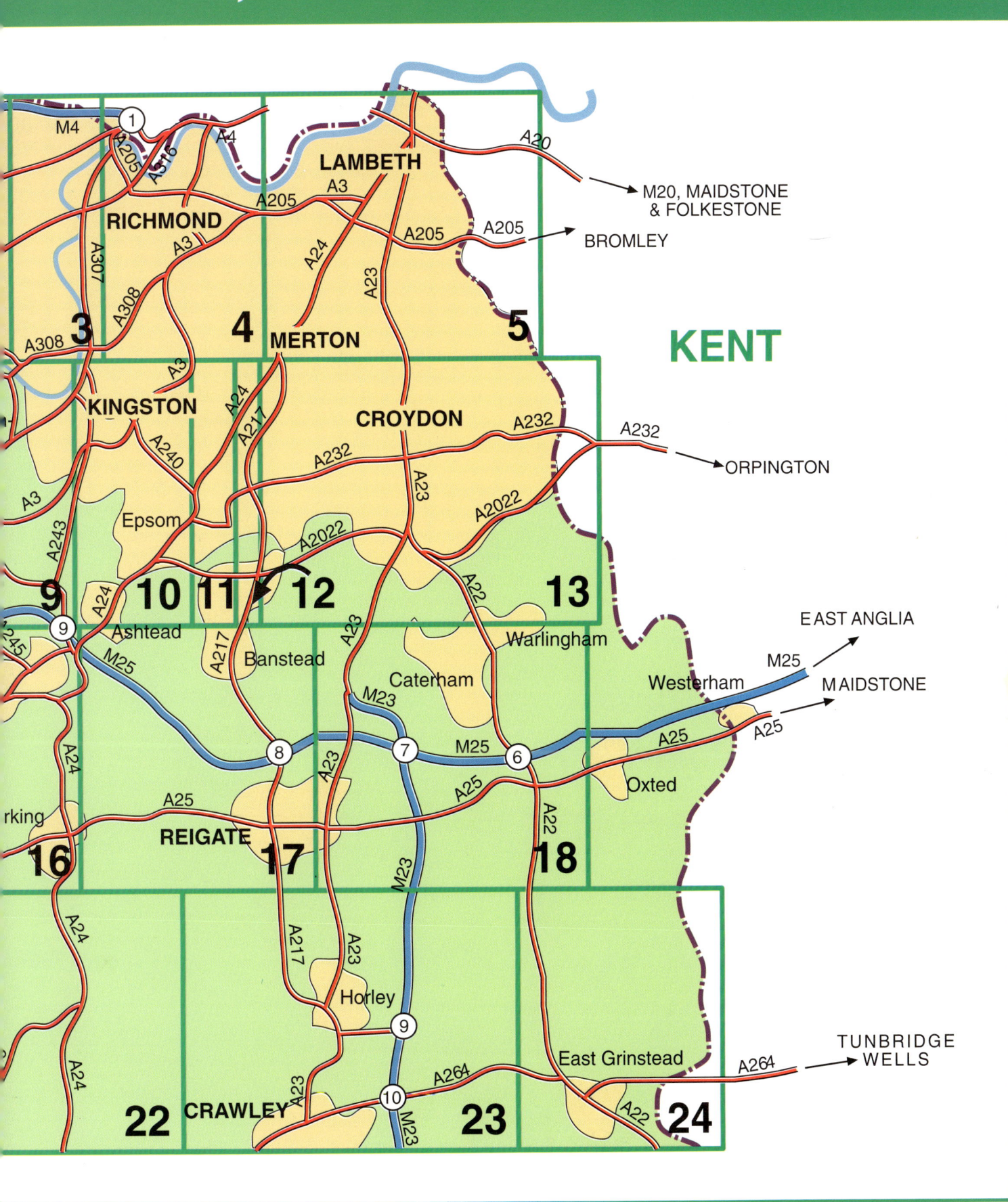

KENT

Road Atlas for Gardeners

MAP PAGES

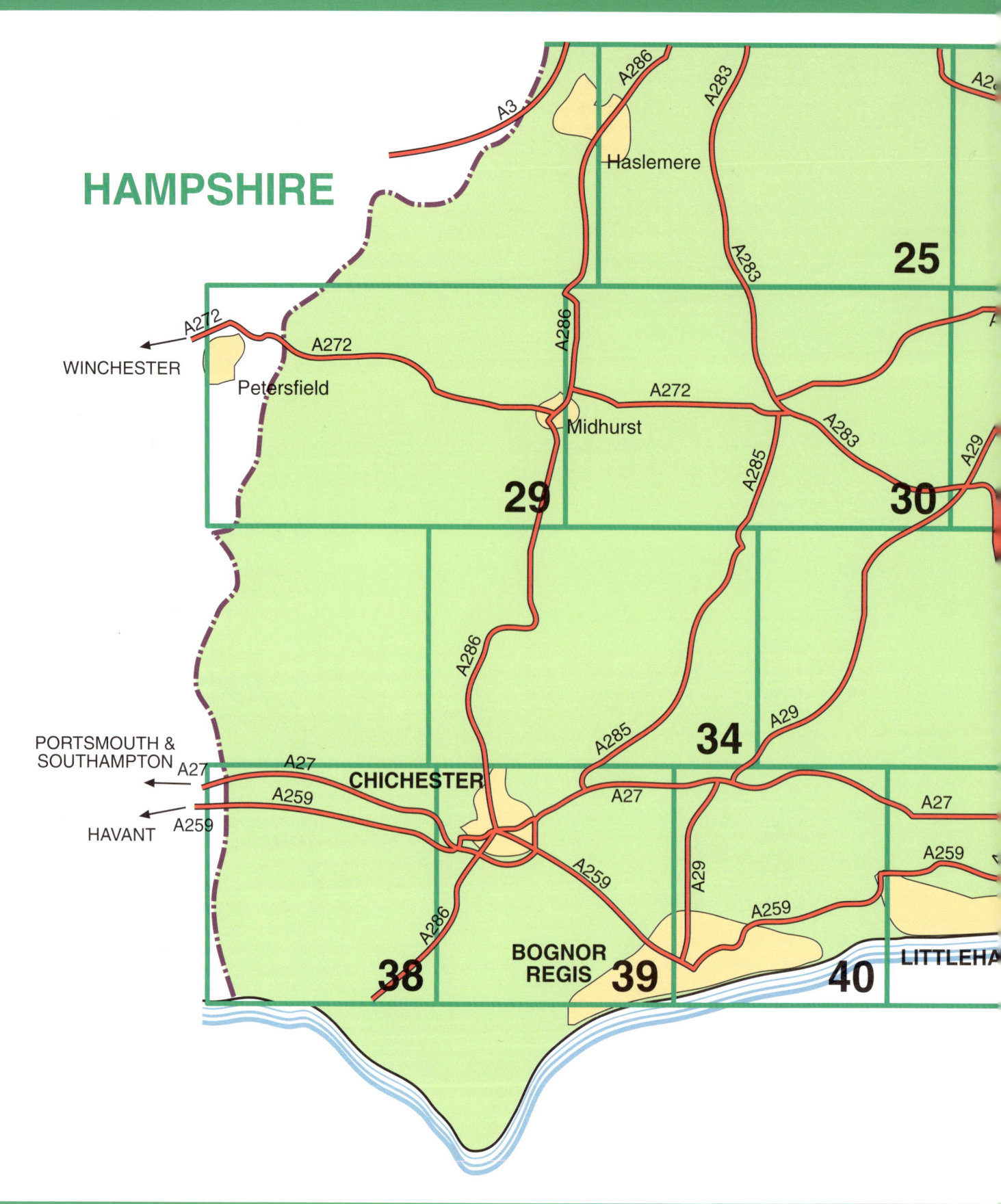

HAMPSHIRE

Road Atlas for Gardeners

WEST SUSSEX

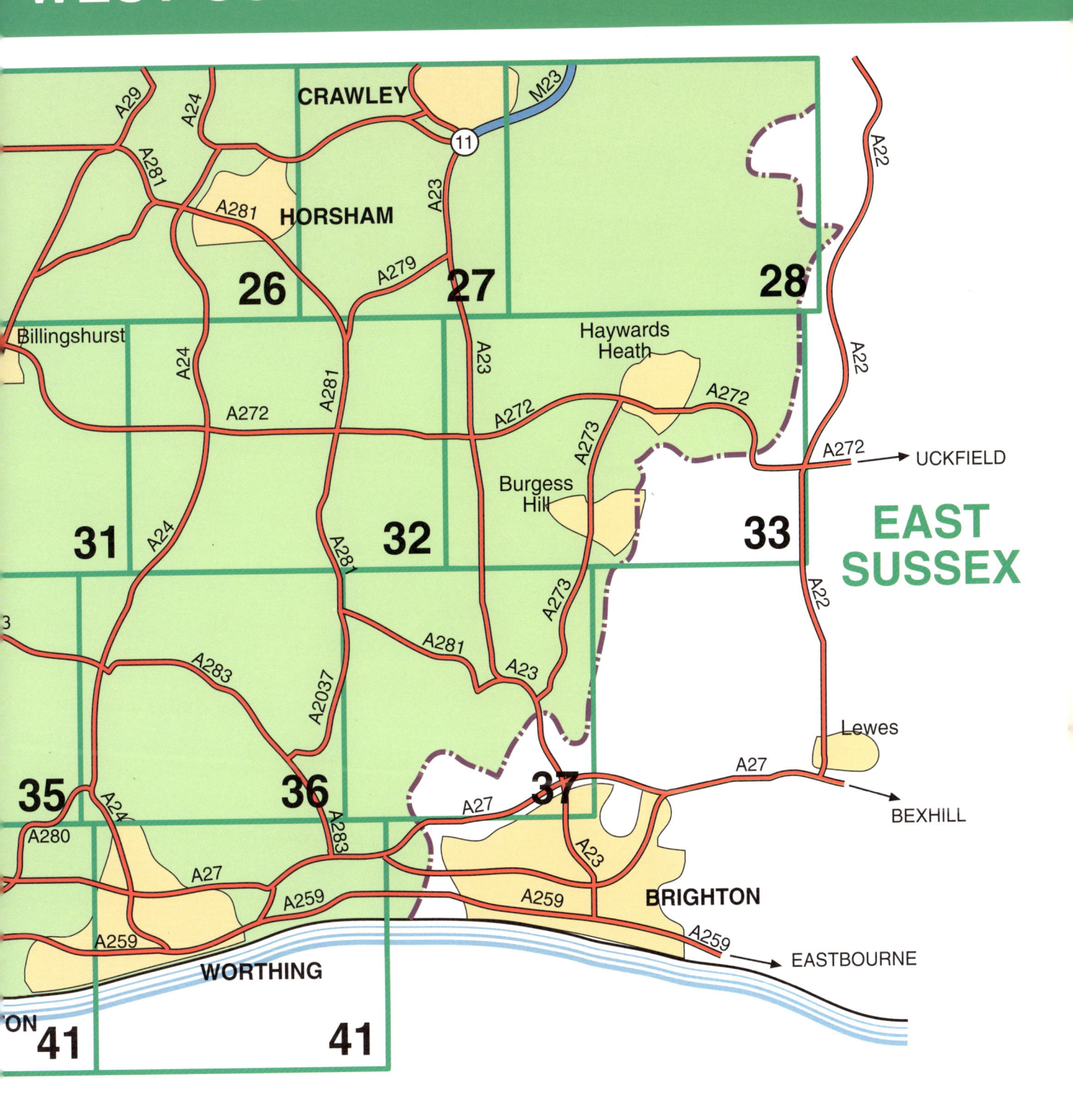

Road Atlas for Gardeners

WEST MIDDLESEX & SURREY

WATER GARDEN CENTRE

1/1 WATERLIFE
Bath Road, Longford,
West Drayton, Middlesex UB7 0ED
01753 – 685 696

NURSERIES & GARDEN CENTRES

1/2 JOHN TRAIN PLANTS
Harmondsworth Road,
West Drayton, Middlesex UB7 9JR
0181 – 759 3010

1/3 VERMEULEN'S GARDEN CENTRE
Horton Road, Stanwell Moor,
Staines, Middlesex TW19 6AE
01784 – 451 737
Large garden centre with a wide selection of plants, rocks, fencing and aquatics. Coffee shop & craft centre.
Open: All year except Christmas and Boxing Days. 7 days a week, Mondays – Saturdays 8.30 – 5.30, Sundays 9.30 – 5.30.
Wheelchairs: Easy access with wide pathways.
Toilets: Yes. **Dogs:** On lead. **Credit cards:** Yes.

1/4 FRANK FAIRHEAD & SON LTD
Bulldog Nurseries,
Town Lane, London Road,
Staines, Middlesex TW19 7JR
01784 – 254 545

1/5 FRANK FAIRHEAD & SON LTD
Greenfield Nurseries, Ashford Road,
Laleham,
Staines, Middlesex TW18 1RS
01784 – 252 620

1/6 NOTCUTTS GARDEN CENTRE
Bloomingdales, Staines Road,
Laleham, Middlesex TW18 2SF
01784 – 460 832

1/7 EGHAM GARDEN CENTRE
Vicarage Road,
Egham, Surrey TW20 8NT
01784 – 433 388

1/8 MAYFLOWER NURSERIES
Thorpe Lea Road,
Egham, Surrey TW20 8JL
01784 – 422 945

GARDENS

1/9 VIRGINIA WATER
London Road,
Virginia Water, Surrey
Costs: Free, but car park charge of £1.30.

1/10 VALLEY GARDENS
Wick Road, Englefield Green,
Egham, Surrey
Costs: Free, but car park charge of £2.60.

1/11 SAVILL GARDEN
Wick Lane, Englefield Green,
Egham, Surrey
Open: All year except Christmas and Boxing Days, 7 days a week, March – October 10 – 6, November – February 10 – 4.
Costs: Adults, £3.30; children, free if accompanied; senior citizens, £2.80.

SEE PAGE 43 FOR FULL DETAILS

Road Atlas for Gardeners

EGHAM & HEATHROW AREA   1

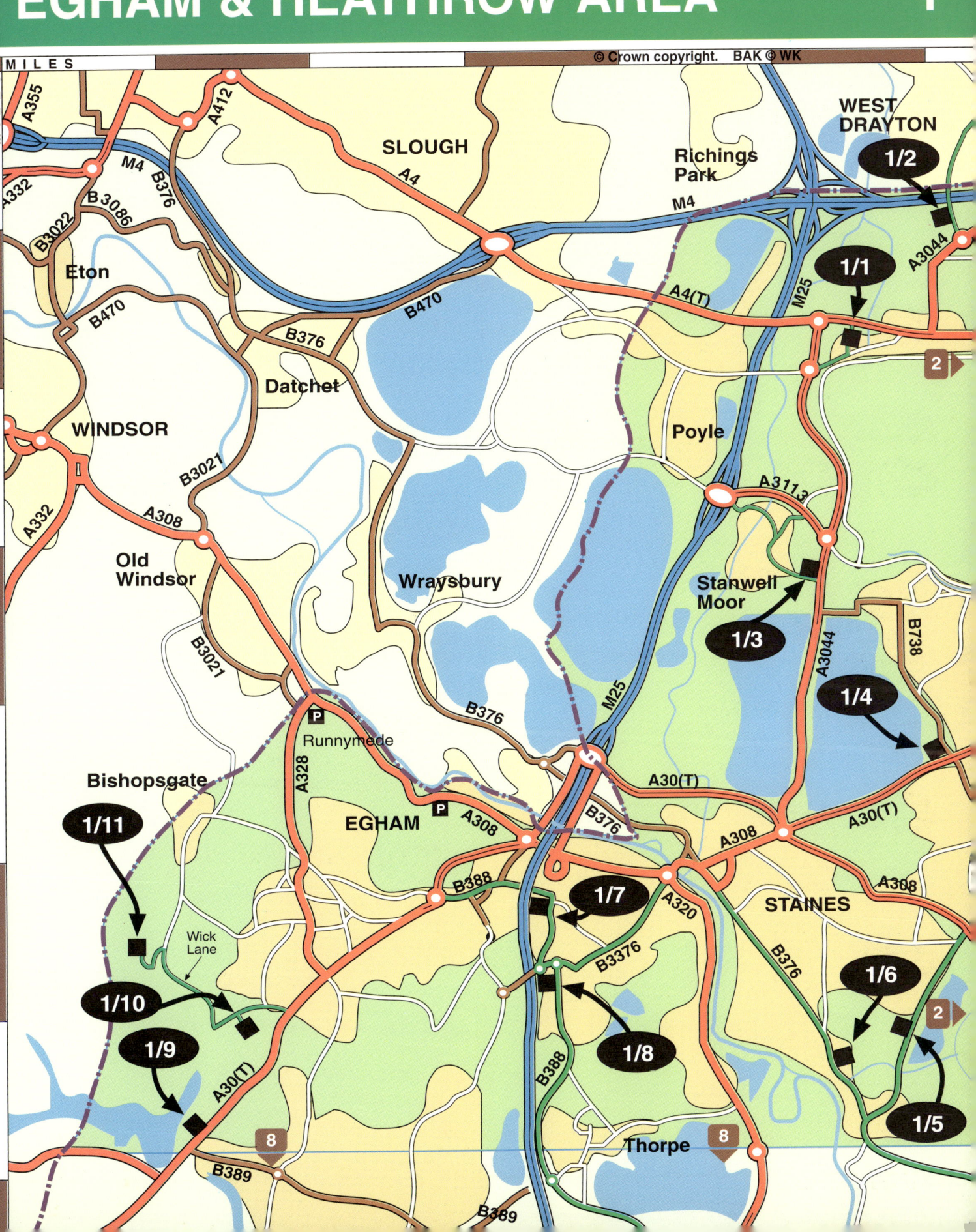

WEST MIDDLESEX

NURSERIES & GARDEN CENTRES

2/1 HEATHROW GARDEN CENTRE
Sipson Road, Sipson,
Near West Drayton, Middlesex UB7 0HP
0181 – 897 8893

2/2 WYEVALE GARDEN CENTRE
Holloway Lane,
West Drayton, Middlesex UB7 0AD
0181 – 897 6075

2/3 PANNELLS GARDEN CENTRE
New Heston Road,
Heston, Middlesex TW5 0RH
0181 – 570 4602

2/4 LAKESIDE GARDEN CENTRE
Bedfont Road,
Feltham, Middlesex TW14 8EA
0181 – 844 2261

2/5 ADRIAN HALL
The Garden Centre,
Feltham Hill Road,
Feltham,
Middlesex
TW13 7NA
0181 – 890 5057

Established 30 years. A 4.5-acre specialist garden centre with vast garden construction materials department.
Open: All year. Mondays – Saturdays 8 – 5.30 (Bank Holidays 9 – 5), Sundays 10 – 4.
Wheelchairs: Level site with good access. A wheelchair is available and there are disabled toilets.
Toilets: Yes.   **Dogs:** On lead.   **Credit cards:** Yes.

SEE PAGE 43 FOR FULL DETAILS

2/6 HOUNSLOW GARDEN CENTRE
462 Staines Road,
Hounslow, Middlesex TW4 5DS
0181 – 572 3211

2/7 SQUIRE'S GARDEN CENTRE
Sixth Cross Road,
Twickenham,
Middlesex
TW2 5PA
0181 – 977 9241

A fine garden centre in the Richmond area. Also café, pets, florist, mowers, health foods, sheds, calor gas.
Open: All year except Christmas and Boxing Days: Mondays – Saturdays 9 – 6 (late nights in Spring), Sundays 10.30 – 4.30.
Wheelchairs: Yes.
Toilets: Yes.   **Dogs:** On lead.   **Credit cards:** Yes.

2/8 GREAT MILLS
Twickenham, Middlesex.

2/9 HOMEBASE

GARDENS

2/10 OSTERLEY PARK (NT)

Open: Grounds open all year, daily 9 – 7.30 or sunset if earlier.
Costs: Free, but car park (closed Christmas and New Year's Days) £1.50.

2/11 THE WALLED GARDEN

Open: All year, 8 – 8 or dusk if earlier.
Cost: Free.

HEATHROW – TWICKENHAM 2

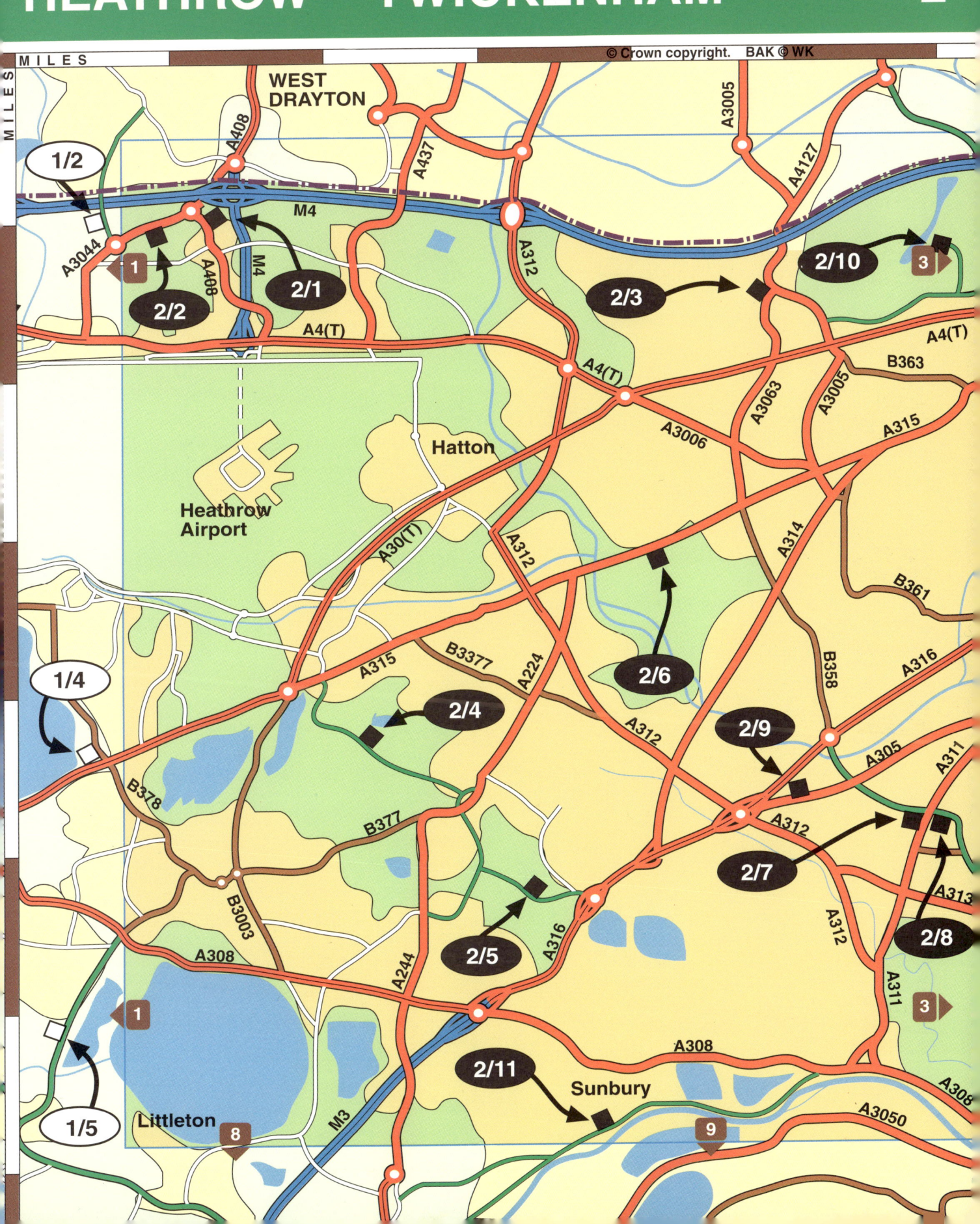

WEST MIDDLESEX

NURSERIES & GARDEN CENTRES

3/1 OSTERLEY GARDEN CENTRE
Windmill Lane,
Osterley, Middlesex TW7 5PP
0181 – 847 2468

3/2 HOMEBASE

3/3 PETERSHAM NURSERIES
Petersham Road,
Petersham,
Richmond,
Surrey TW10 7AG
0181 – 940 5230

Grower of quality bedding plants and large selection of shrubs and trees. Very close to Richmond Park.
Open: All year except Christmas, Boxing and New Year's Days. 7 days a week, Mondays – Saturdays 9 – 5.30, Sundays 10 – 4.
Wheelchairs: All plant areas accessible.
Toilets: Ask if desperate. **Dogs:** On lead.
Credit cards: Yes.

3/4 TEDDINGTON STATION GARDEN CENTRE
Station Road,
Teddington, Middlesex TW11 9AB
0181 – 943 5222

GARDENS

3/5 HAM HOUSE (NT)

Open: Garden all year except Christmas, Boxing and New Year's Days. 6 days a week (CLOSED FRIDAYS but open Good Friday), 10.30 – 6 or dusk if earlier.
Costs: Garden free. **Wheelchairs:** Grounds include some steep gravel paths; 2 wheelchairs available. There are disabled toilets.

3/6 WOODLAND GARDENS, BUSHY PARK

Open: All year, daily, 7.30 – dusk.
Costs: Free.

3/7 PALACE GARDENS, HAMPTON COURT

Tudor, Baroque & Victorian gardens. Maze, Great Vine.
Open: All year, 7 days a week, 7 – dusk.
Costs: Gardens free, but parking £1.60.
Maze, adults £1.70, children £1.00.

GARDEN & GARDEN CENTRE

3/8 SYON PARK
Brentford,
Middlesex
TW8 8JF
0181 – 560 0881

55 acres of Capability Brown gardens, at their best in spring and autumn. Great Conservatory.
Open: All year except Christmas and Boxing Days. 7 days a week, 10 – 6 or dusk.
Costs: Adults, £2.50; concessions, £2.00; families, £5.00.
Wheelchairs: Access throughout the gardens. There are disabled toilets.
Toilets: Yes. **Dogs:** No. **Credit cards:** No.

3/9 SYON PARK GARDEN CENTRE
Syon Park,
Brentford, Middlesex TW8 8JG
0181 – 568 0134
Retail garden centre, landscape supplies, garden and design service.
Open: All year except Christmas and Boxing Days. Weekdays 9 – 5.30, Sundays 10.30 – 4.30.
Toilets: Yes. **Dogs:** No. **Credit cards:** Yes.

M4 – HAMPTON COURT   3

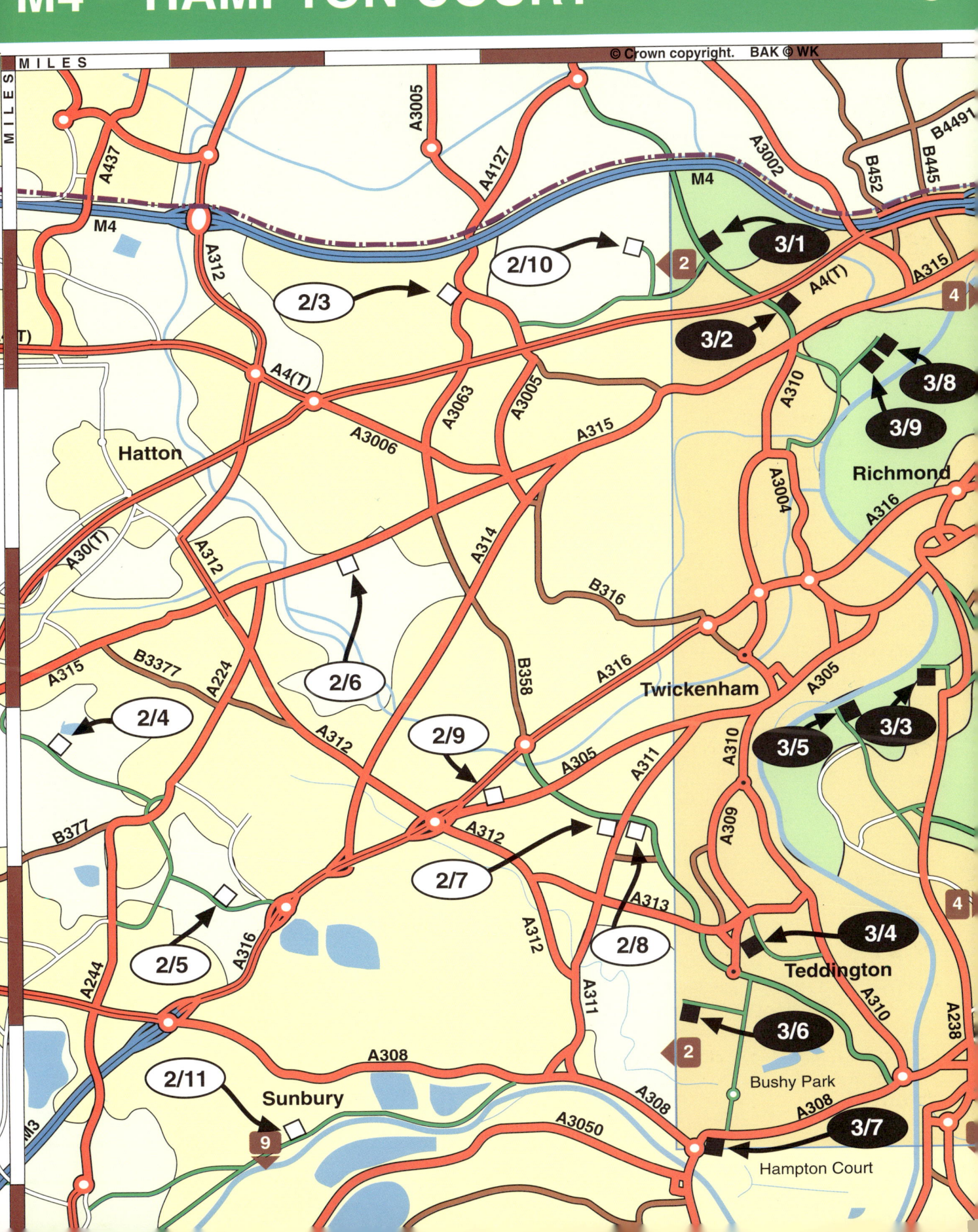

S.W. LONDON

NURSERIES & GARDEN CENTRES

4/1 HOMEBASE

4/2 THE PALM CENTRE
63 Upper Richmond Road, East Sheen, Richmond, Surrey SW14 7EB
0181 – 876 3223

4/3 ROCKINGHAMS GARDEN CENTRE
181 Upper Richmond Road West, East Sheen,
Richmond, Surrey SW14 8DV
0181 – 876 3648

4/4 ADRIAN HALL
Putney Garden Centre,
Dryburgh Road,
Putney, London
SW15 1BN
0181 – 789 9518

Wide selection of products and plants for the London garden. Pots, containers and trellis are specialities.
Open: All year. Mondays – Saturdays 9 – 5.30, Sundays and Bank Holidays 10 – 4.
Toilets: Yes. **Dogs:** On lead. **Credit cards:** Yes.

4/5 HOMEBASE

4/6 B & Q

GARDENS

4/7 ROYAL BOTANIC GARDENS, KEW
Richmond,
Surrey
TW9 3AB
0181 – 940 1171

The world's leading botanic garden and plant research centre.
Open: All year except Christmas & New Year's Days. 7 days a week, 9.30 – dusk.
Costs: Adults, £4.00; children, £2.00; concessions, £2.00; families, £10.00.
Wheelchairs: Easy access to most areas. Wheelchairs are available and tours can be pre-booked in a special bus for the disabled.
Toilets: Yes. **Dogs:** No. **Credit cards:** Yes.

4/8 ISABELLA PLANTATION, RICHMOND PARK
Open: All year. 7 days a week, 7.30 – dusk.
Costs: Free.

Royal Botanic Gardens, Kew

Road Atlas for Gardeners

RICHMOND – WIMBLEDON 4

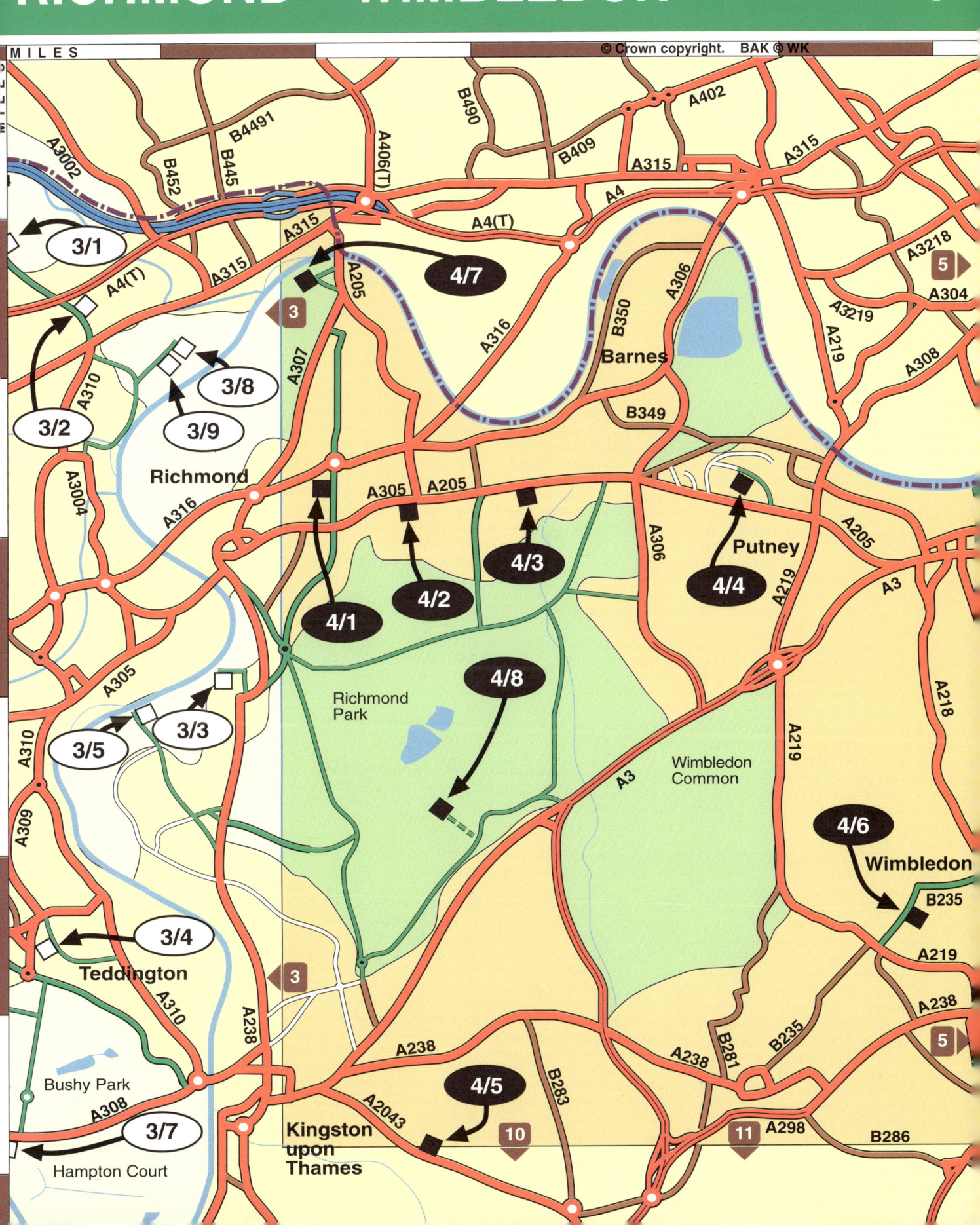

S.W. LONDON

NURSERIES & GARDEN CENTRES

5/1 B & Q

5/2 HOMEBASE

5/3 HOMEBASE

5/4 BRYAN'S GARDEN CENTRE
100 Tooting Bec Road,
Wandsworth,
London
SW17 8BG
0181–672 2251

Specialists in flowering evergreens, climbers, roses, bedding and herbaceous plants, herbs, house plants. Statuary.
Open: All year except Christmas. Open Easter Sunday. 7 days a week. Winter: weekdays 9 – dusk, Sundays 9.30 – dusk. Summer: weekdays 9 – 6, Sundays 9.30 – 6.
Toilets: No.   **Dogs:** On lead.   **Credit cards:** Yes.

Paul Temple

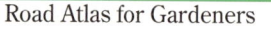

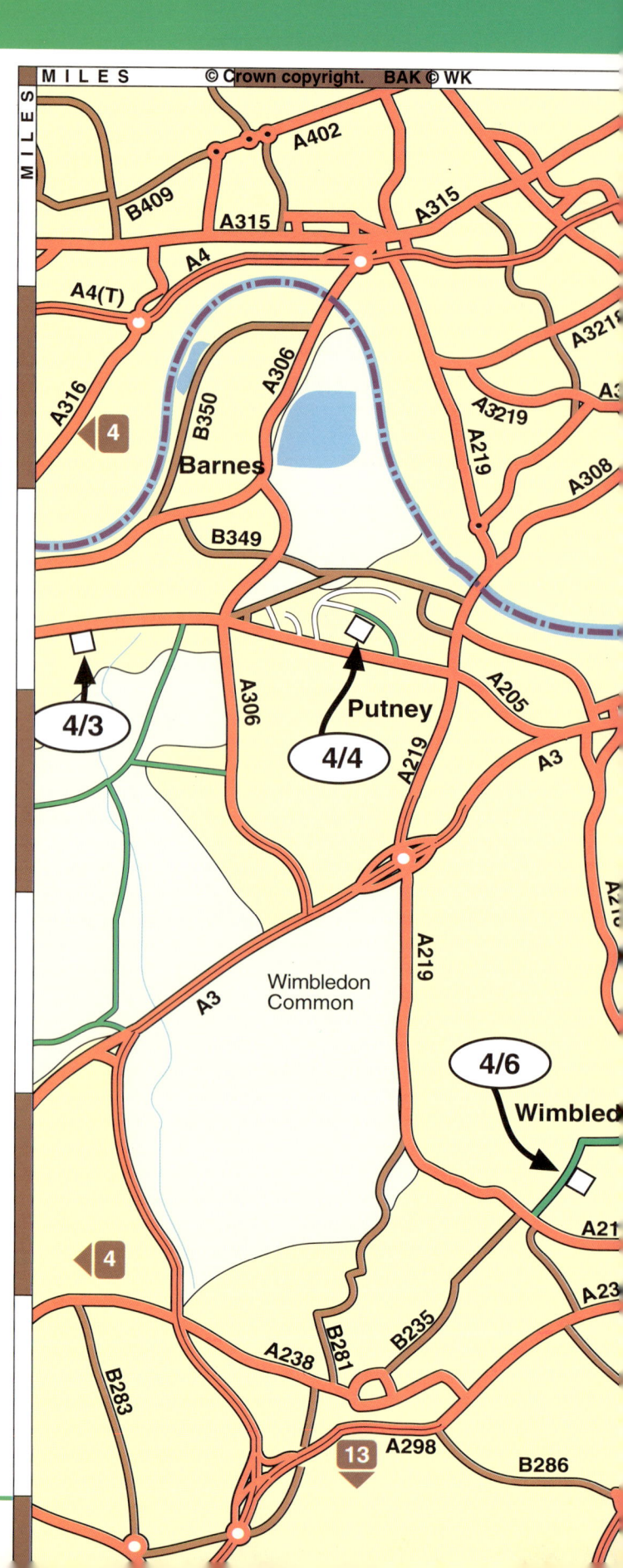

Road Atlas for Gardeners

WANDSWORTH – STREATHAM 5

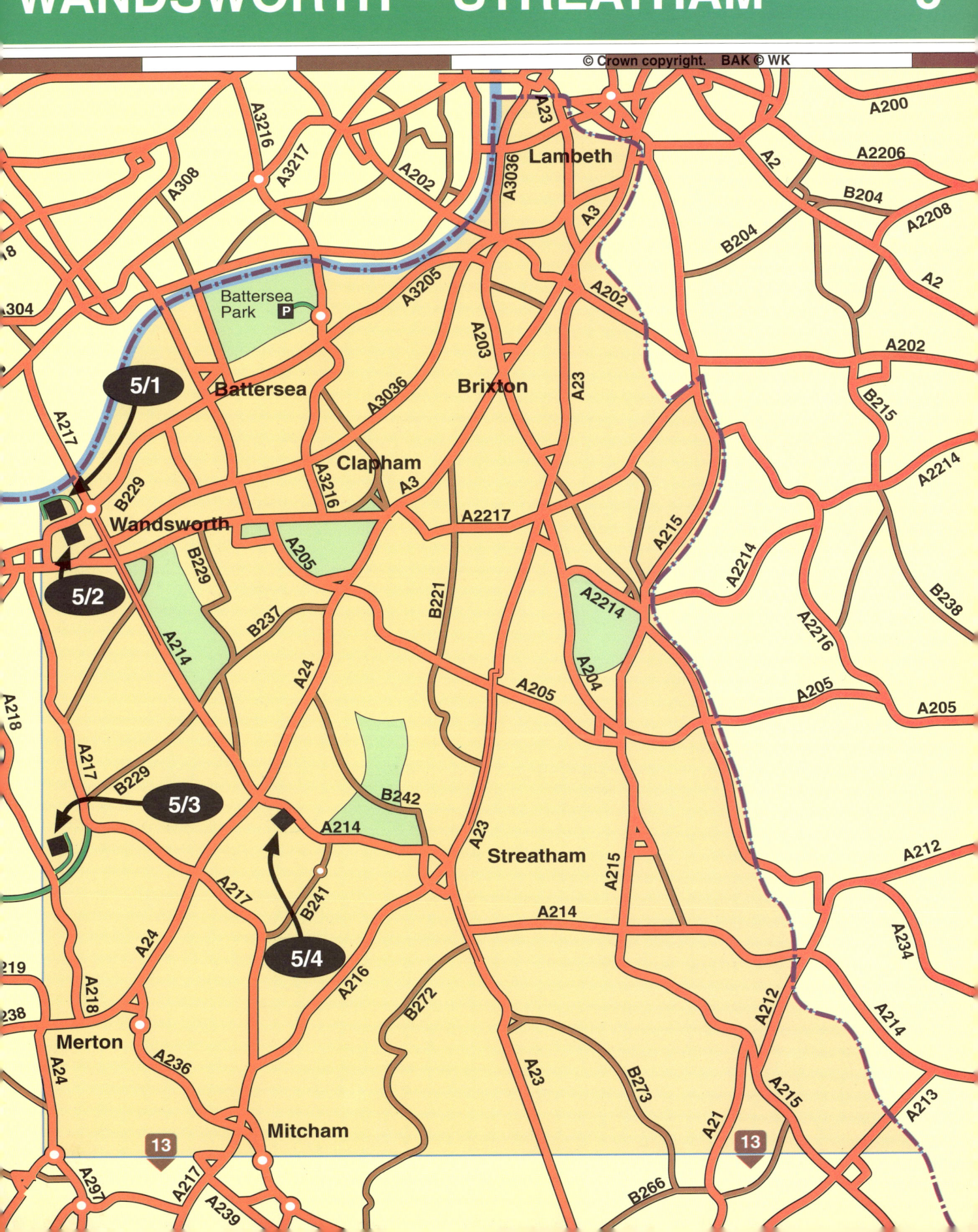

SURREY

NURSERIES & GARDEN CENTRES

6/1 NURSERY COURT GARDENS
Nursery Court, London Road,
Windlesham, Surrey GU20 6LQ

6/2 HILLIER GARDEN CENTRE
Sunningdale Nurseries, London Road,
Windlesham, Surrey GU20 6LM
01344 – 23166

6/3 COUNTRY GARDEN CENTRE

6/4 LONGACRES NURSERY
London Road,
Bagshot, Surrey GU19 5JB
01276 – 476 778

6/5 NOTCUTTS WATERERS NURSERIES
150 London Road,
Bagshot, Surrey GU19 5DC
01276 – 472 288

6/6 HOMEBASE

6/7 COPPED HALL COTTAGE GARDENS
Stonegate,
Camberley, Surrey GU15 1PC
01276–22468

6/8 BROOK NURSERY
163 Guildford Road, West End,
Woking, Surrey GU24 9LS
01483 – 473 147

6/9 LINCLUDEN NURSERY
Bisley Green, Bisley,
Woking, Surrey GU24 9EN
01483 – 797 005

Dwarf, slow-growing & unusual conifers. Large selection of shrubs, climbers etc. Chelsea Flower Show exhibitor.
Open: All year except 20 – 30 May, 12 – 26 June, 22 December – 5 January. 6 days a week (CLOSED SUNDAYS), 9.30 – 4.30.
Toilets: Yes.   **Dogs:** No.   **Credit cards:** Yes.

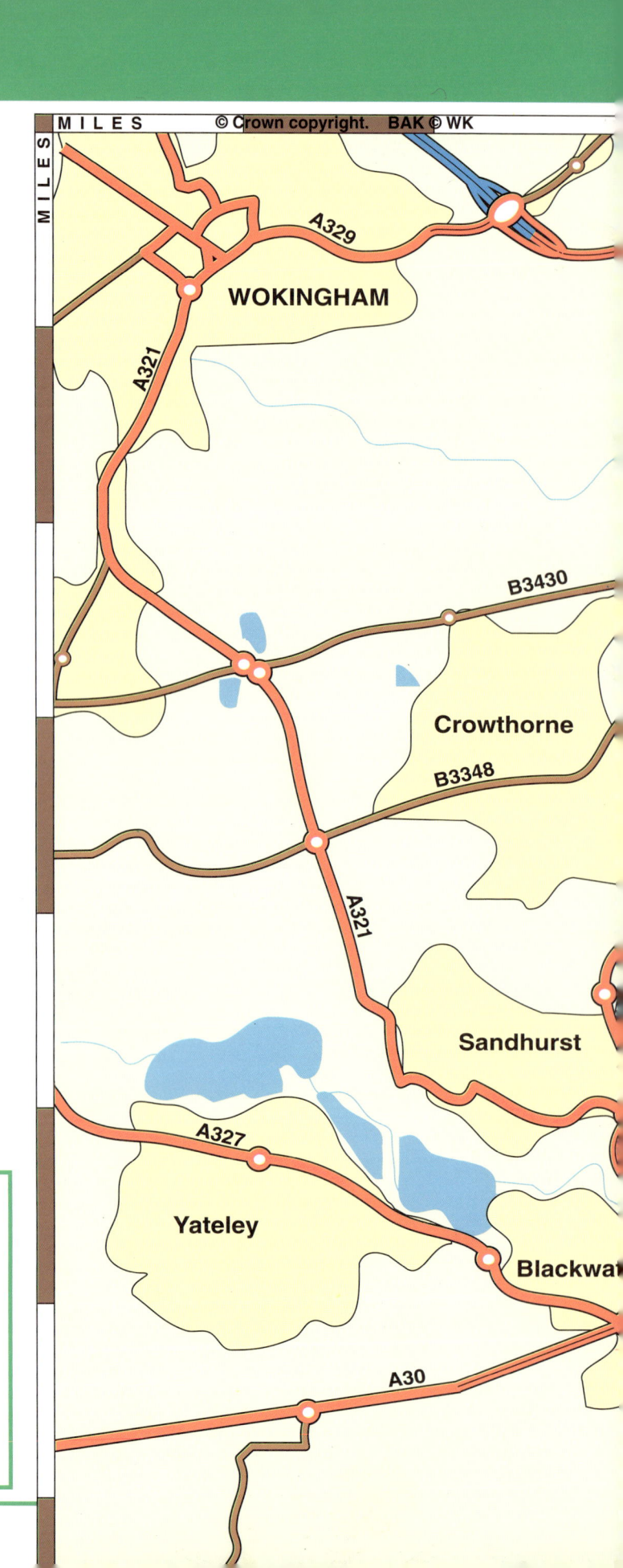

Road Atlas for Gardeners

CAMBERLEY AREA 6

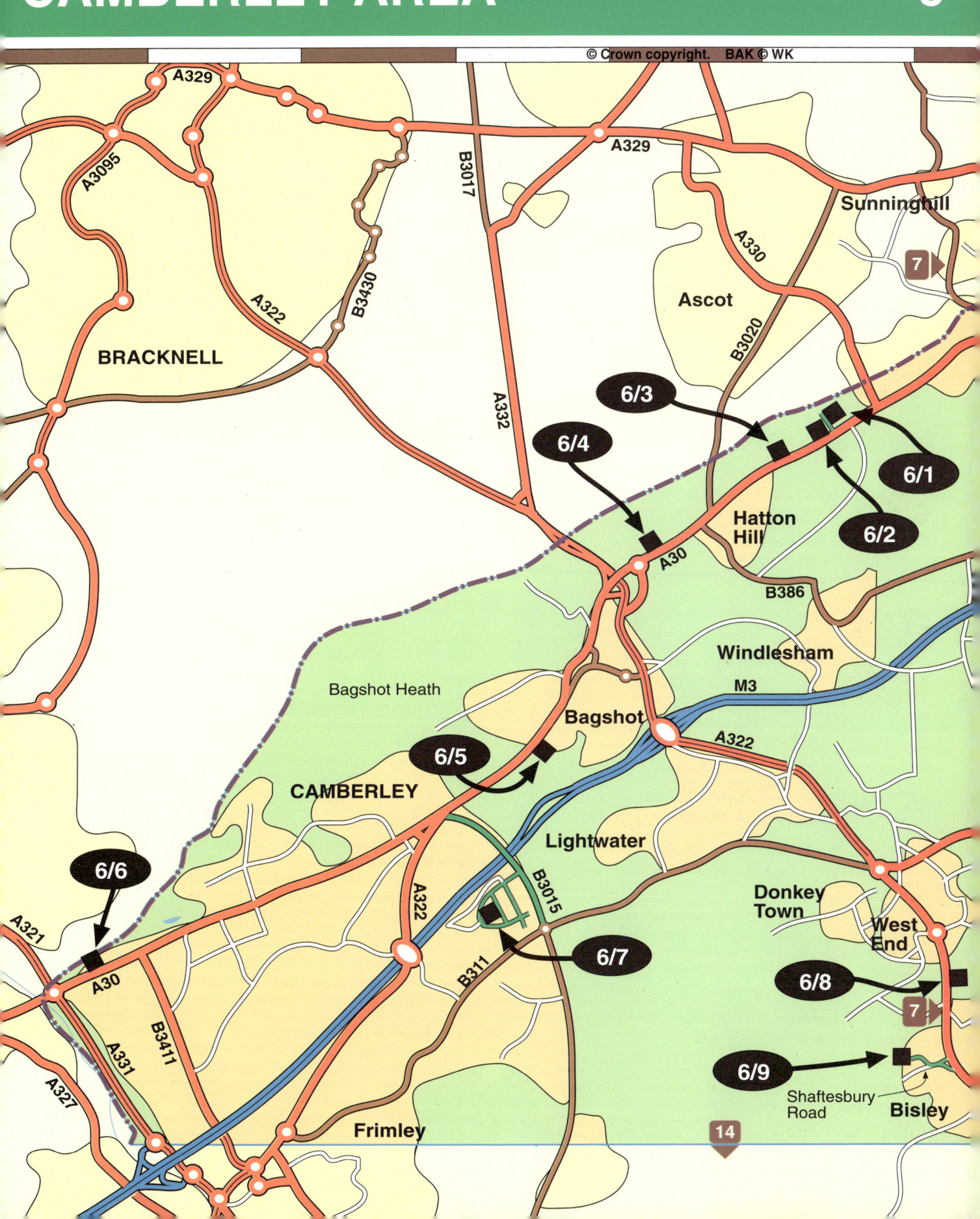

SURREY

NURSERIES & GARDEN CENTRES

7/1 PANTILES NURSERIES
Almners Road,
Lyne,
Chertsey, Surrey
KT16 0BJ
01932 – 872 195

'Instant gardens' – large and unusual conifers, trees and shrubs – 3-litre containers up to 1200 litres.
Open: All year except Christmas, Boxing and New Year's Days. Mondays – Saturdays 8.30–5.30, Sundays 9–5.
Wheelchairs: Easy paved access.
Toilets: Yes.   **Dogs:** On lead.   **Credit cards:** Yes.

7/2 THE PLANT CENTRE
Bagshot Road,
Chobham,
Woking, Surrey
GU24 8SJ
01276 – 855 408

Plant centre with extensive range of own-grown trees and shrubs, both popular and unusual.
Open: All year except Christmas Day. 7 days a week, 8.30 – 6 or dusk in winter.
Wheelchairs: Good paved access.
Toilets: Yes.   **Dogs:** No.   **Credit cards:** Yes.

7/3 CHOBHAM NURSERIES
Bagshot Road,
Chobham, Surrey   GU24 8DF
01276 – 858 252

7/4 RIVERSIDE NURSERIES
Philpot Lane, Chobham,
Woking, Surrey   GU24 8HE
01276 – 857 687

A nursery specialising in bedding plants, summer and winter hanging baskets, winter pansies and bulbs.
Open: All year except Christmas, Boxing and New Year's Days. 7 days a week March – June and September – November, 9 – 5. Other months closed Sundays.
Wheelchairs: Easy paved access.
Toilets: No.   **Dogs:** Yes.   **Credit cards:** No.

7/5 MIMBRIDGE GARDEN CENTRE
Station Road, Chobham,
Woking, Surrey   GU24 8AR
01276 – 858 237

7/6 KNAPHILL GARDEN CENTRE
Barrs Lane, Knaphill,
Woking, Surrey   GU21 2JW
01483 – 481 212

7/7 SQUIRE'S GARDEN CENTRE

Littlewick Road,
Horsell, Woking,
Surrey   GU21 4XR
01276 – 858 446

This garden centre, close to Woking and Chobham, is expanding and will be enlarged during 1995.
Open: All year except Christmas and Boxing Days. 7 days a week, 9 – 6.
Wheelchairs: Most of the area is paved.
Toilets: New toilets in late 1995.   **Dogs:** On lead.
Credit cards: Yes.

Road Atlas for Gardeners

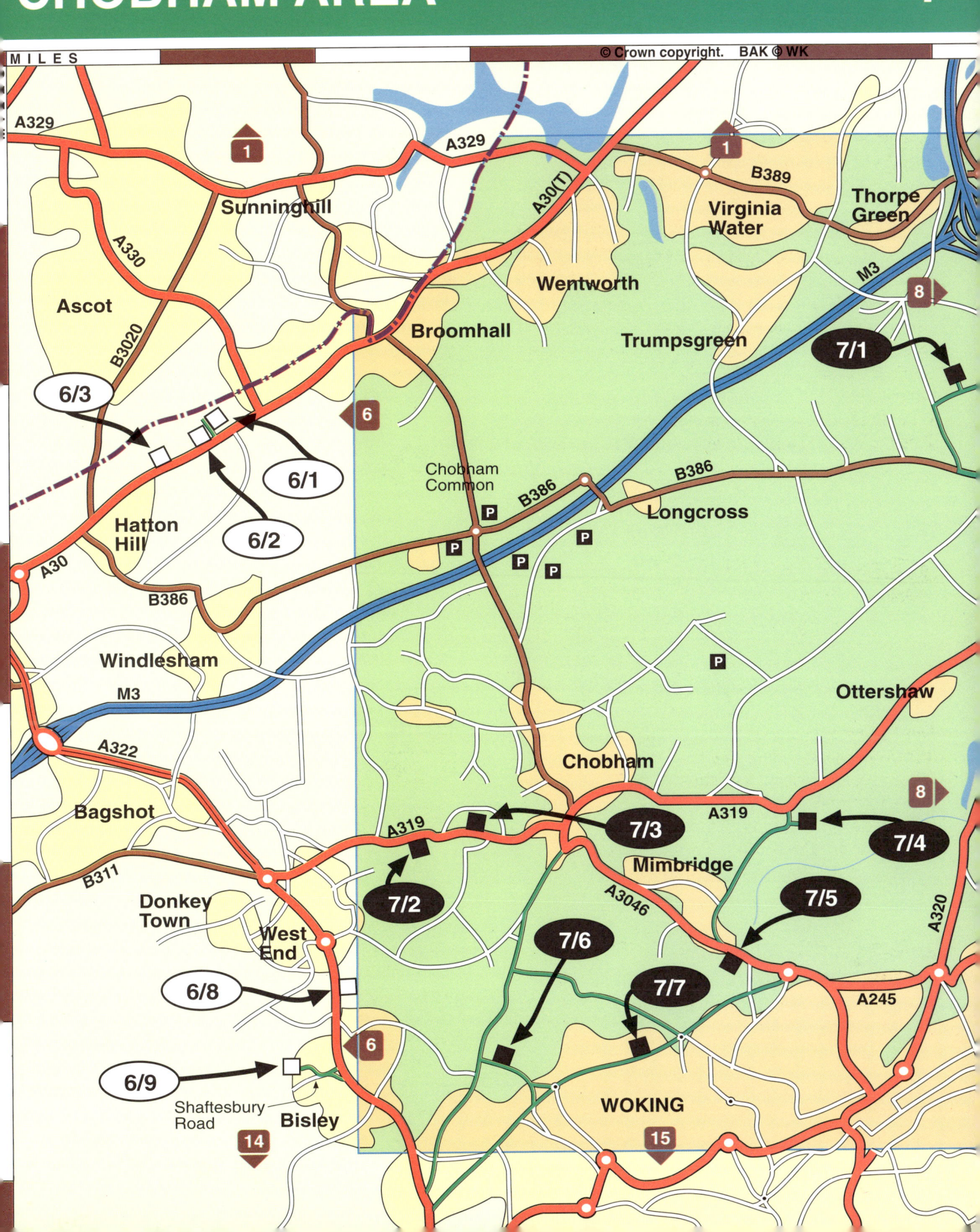

CHOBHAM AREA 7

SURREY

NURSERIES & GARDEN CENTRES

8/1 LALEHAM NURSERIES
Laleham Road,
Shepperton, Middlesex
01932 – 563 322

8/2 SQUIRE'S GARDEN CENTRE
Halliford Road,
Upper Halliford,
Shepperton,
Middlesex
TW17 8RU
Garden centre 01932 – 784 121
Nursery 01932 – 783 219
Garden centre and rose nursery, craft shop, café, farm shop, mowers, wool shop. Sheds and conservatories.
Open: All year except Christmas and Boxing Days. 7 days a week, Mondays – Saturdays 9 – 6, Sundays 10.30 – 4.30 (late nights in spring).
Wheelchairs: Yes.
Toilets: Yes. **Dogs:** On lead. **Credit cards:** Yes.

8/3 THE HIDDEN GARDEN
Nutty Lane,
Shepperton, Middlesex TW17 0RQ
01932 – 781 474

8/4 JUNGLE GARDEN CENTRE
Fordbridge Road,
Sunbury on Thames, Middx TW16 6AY
01932 – 772 136

8/5 THE NURSERY
Hardwick Lane,
Lyne, Surrey

8/6 WOBURN HILL NURSERY
Woburn Hill, Addlestone,
Weybridge, Surrey KT15 2QE
01932 – 821 066

8/7 CROCKFORD PARK GARDEN CENTRE
40 Crockford Park Road,
Addlestone, Surrey KT15 2LY
01932 – 847 647

8/8 THE OTTER NURSERY
Murray Road,
Ottershaw, Surrey KT16 0HT
01932 – 874 875

8/9 BOURNE VALLEY GARDEN CENTRE
Woodham Park Road, Woodham,
Weybridge, Surrey KT15 3TJ
01932 – 342 013

8/10 JACQUES CANN OF WEYBRIDGE
Hillview Nursery, Seven Hills Road,
Walton-on-Thames, Surrey KT12 4DD
01932 – 844 575

8/11 HOMEBASE

8/12 SQUIRE'S GARDEN CENTRE
Holloway Hill,
Chertsey,
Surrey KT16 0AE
01932 – 563 727
Attractive compact garden centre in lodge setting. Garden buildings.
Open: All year except Christmas and Boxing Days. 7 days a week, 9 – 6.
Wheelchairs: Yes.
Toilets: Yes. **Dogs:** On lead. **Credit cards:** Yes.

WATER GARDEN CENTRE

8/13 WORLD OF WATER
Holloway Hill,
Chertsey, Surrey KT16 0AE
01932 – 569 690
Specialists in water gardens, fountains, filtration, fish, plants and everything for the garden pond.
Open: All year except Christmas, Boxing and New Year's Days. 7 days a week 9 – 6. November – January, 6 days a week (CLOSED SUNDAYS).
Wheelchairs: Easy paved access.
Toilets: Yes. **Dogs:** Yes. **Credit cards:** Yes.

GARDEN

8/14 PAINSHILL PARK

Open: 9 April – 15 October 1995, Sundays only, 11–5.
Costs: Adults, £3.50; children over 5, £2.00; senior citizens and disabled, £3.00.

Road Atlas for Gardeners

WEYBRIDGE AREA 8

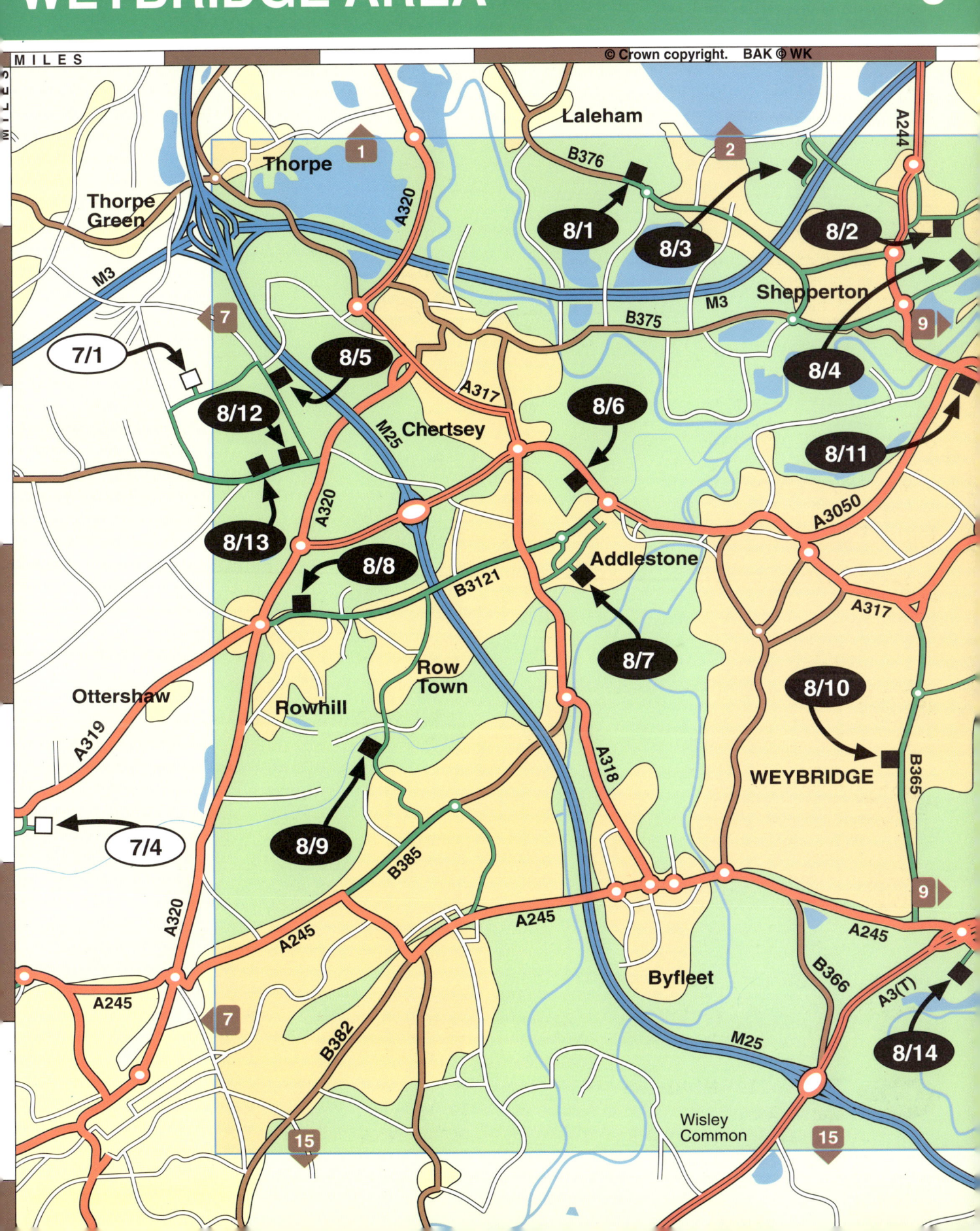

SURREY

NURSERIES & GARDEN CENTRES

9/1 SQUIRE'S GARDEN CENTRE
Burwood Road,
Hersham,
Surrey KT12 4AR
01932 – 247 579

Set in a Victorian farm complex. Café, wide range of garden furniture, garden pots and statues; sheds.
Open: All year except Christmas and Boxing Days. Mondays – Saturdays 9 – 6, Sundays 10.30 – 4.30.
Wheelchairs: Yes.
Toilets: Yes.   **Dogs:** On lead.   **Credit cards:** Yes.

9/2 HILL PARK ROSES
Woodstock Lane North,
Surbiton, Surrey KT6 5HM
0181 – 398 0022

9/3 WOODSTOCK GARDEN CENTRE
Woodstock Lane North,
Surbiton, Surrey KT6 5HN
0181 – 398 6040/7170

9/4 KENNEDYS GARDEN CENTRE
Oaken Lane, Claygate, Surrey KT10 0RH
0181 – 398 0047

9/5 CHESSINGTON GARDEN CENTRE
Leatherhead Road,
Chessington, Surrey KT9 2NF
01372 – 725 638

9/6 COBHAM PARK NURSERY
Plough Lane, Downside,
Cobham, Surrey KT11 3LU
01932 – 863 933

Nursery in walled garden, growing all own general stock, summer bedding and herbaceous perennials.
Open: All year except Christmas Day. 6 days a week (CLOSED WEDNESDAYS), 10 – 5.
Wheelchairs: Reasonably paved access.
Toilets: No.   **Dogs:** On lead.   **Credit cards:** No.

9/7 WILLOUGHBY'S NURSERIES
Leatherhead Road,
Oxshott, Surrey KT22 0HC
01372 – 842 434

9/8 PETERS PLANTS & GARDEN CENTRE
Stoke Road,
Stoke D'Abernon,
Cobham,
Surrey KT11 3PU
01932 – 862 530

Large 5-acre garden centre in a beautiful setting thoroughly plant orientated with landscape, gift depts & much more.
Open: All year except Christmas holidays. Monday–Saturday 9 – 5.30 (till 5 winter months), Sundays 9.45–4.
Wheelchairs: Good paved access and ramps.
Toilets: Yes.   **Dogs:** On lead.   **Credit cards:** Yes.

PICK-YOUR-OWN FARM & GARDEN CENTRE

9/9 GARSON FARM
Winterdown Road,
West End, Esher,
Surrey KT10 8LS
Garden Centre 01372 – 460 181
PYO 01372 – 464 389

A large range of fruit and vegetables to pick from May to October and a large modern garden centre.
Open: All year except Xmas & Boxing Days & Easter Sunday. 7 days a week. Winter: Mon – Thur 9 – 5, Fri 9 – 6, Sat 9 – 5, Sun 10.30 – 4.30. Summer: Mon – Sat 9 – 6; Sundays, garden centre 10.30 – 4.30, PYO 9 – 7.
Wheelchairs: Good access including disabled toilets.
Toilets: Yes.   **Dogs:** On lead (but not in PYO fields).
Credit cards: Garden centre, yes; PYO, no.

PICK-YOUR-OWN FARM

9/10 CHURCH FARM
Burhill Road,
Hersham, Surrey KT12 4BK
01932 – 242 212

GARDEN

9/11 CLAREMONT GARDEN (NT)

Open: All year. January – end March, 6 days a week (CLOSED MONDAYS) 10 – 5 or sunset if earlier. April – end October, Mon – Fri 10 – 6, Sat, Sun & Bank Holiday Mondays 10 – 7. (12 – 16 JULY GARDEN CLOSES AT 4.)
Costs: Adults, Mon – Sat £1.80, Sun and Bank Hols £2.60.   **Wheelchairs:** Level pathway around lake, level grassland. Wheelchairs available. Disabled toilets.

Road Atlas for Gardeners

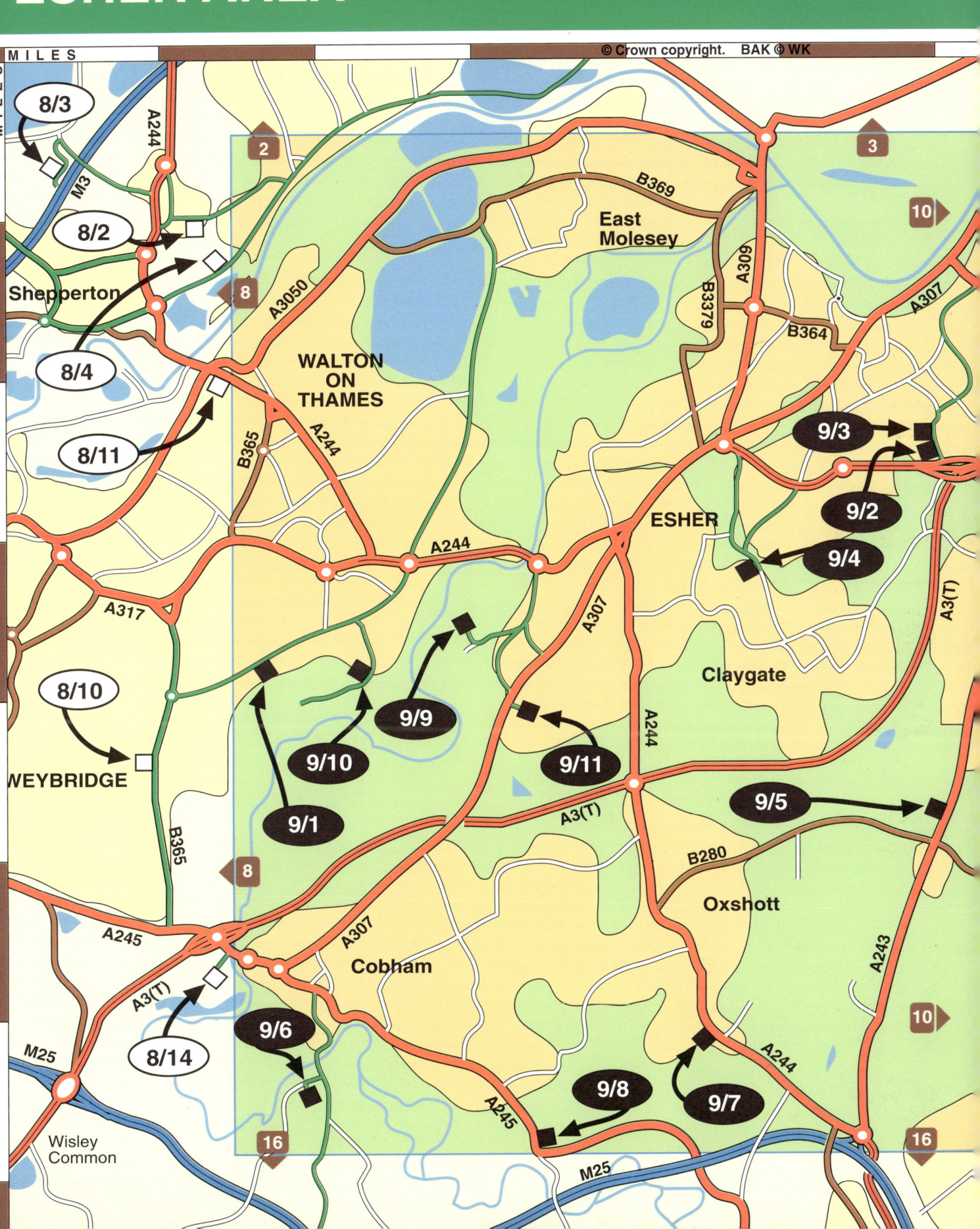

ESHER AREA 9

SURREY

WATER GARDEN CENTRE

10/1 EGMONT WATER GARDEN CENTRE
132 Tolworth Rise South,
Surbiton, Surrey
0181 – 337 9605

NURSERIES & GARDEN CENTRES

10/2 B & Q

10/3 B & Q

10/4 GARDEN CARE SUPPLIES
Old Kingston Road,
Worcester Park, Surrey KT4 7QH
0181 – 337 9922

10/5 SEYMOURS GARDEN & LEISURE CENTRE
The Pit House,
By-pass,
Ewell, Surrey
KT17 1PS
0181 – 393 0111

Well known centre with coffee shop in 18th century listed house sells garden furniture, aquatics, gifts & much more.
Open: All year except Christmas holidays and Easter Sunday. Mondays – Saturdays 9 – 6 (till 7, April – June, till 5 in winter months); Sundays 9.45 – 4.
Wheelchairs: No.
Toilets: Yes.   **Dogs:** On lead.   **Credit cards:** Yes.

10/6 DO IT ALL

10/7 MARSDEN NURSERY AND GARDEN CENTRE
Pleasure Pit Road,
Ashtead, Surrey KT21 1HV
01372 – 273 891

Furniture, barbecues, greenhouses, fruit trees, wide variety of trees, shrubs, conifers and climbers. Garden sundries.
Open: All year except Christmas, Boxing and New Year's Days. 7 days a week, Mondays – Fridays 8 – 5, Saturdays, Sundays and Bank Holidays 9 – 5.
Wheelchairs: Wide doors, ramps, easy access.
Toilets: Yes.   **Dogs:** On lead.   **Credit cards:** Yes.

10/8 FARM LANE NURSERIES
Farm Lane,
Ashtead, Surrey, KT21 1LY
01372 – 274 400

An enthusiastic family nursery, with an interesting and unusual range of plants and shrubs.
Open: All year except 4 days over Christmas. 6 days a week (CLOSED MONDAYS but open 7 days in summer bedding season). Weekdays: 8.30 – 5, Sundays 10 – 5 or dusk in winter.
Toilets: Yes.   **Dogs:** No.   **Credit cards:** Yes.

10/9 D.I.Y. GARDEN CENTRE
Bramley Corner, Epsom Road,
Ashtead, Surrey KT21 1JF
0372 – 273 590

10/10 A. J. DOBBE AND SONS
Bramley Nurseries, Bramley Way,
Ashtead, Surrey KT21 1RD
01372 – 273 924

Old established family run nursery. Specialists in home grown bedding plants, wholesale welcomed. Florist.
Open: All year except Christmas and Boxing Days. 7 days a week, Mondays – Saturdays 8 – 5.30; Sundays 10 – 4.30.
Wheelchairs: No.
Toilets: Ask if desperate.   **Dogs:** On lead.
Credit cards: Yes.

Road Atlas for Gardeners

SURBITON – EPSOM 10

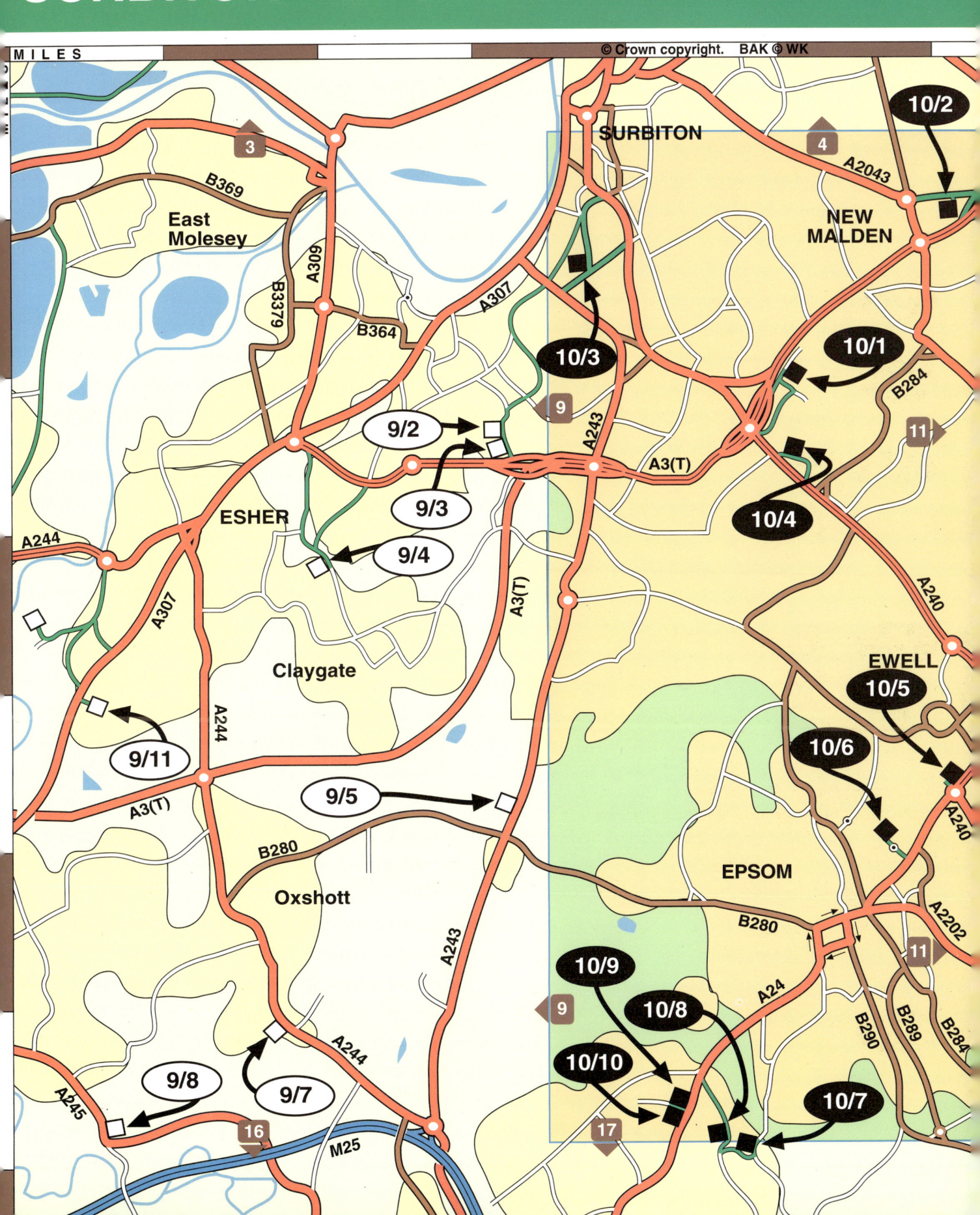

Surrey

GARDEN CENTRE & GARDEN

11/1 MORDEN HALL GARDEN CENTRE
Morden Hall Park,
Morden Hall Road,
Morden, Surrey
SM4 5JD
0181 – 646 3002

A beautiful garden centre in a picturesque setting within an old Elizabethan walled garden. Includes café and National Trust shop.
Open: All year, except Christmas, Boxing and New Year's Days. 7 days a week, weekdays 9 – 5, Sundays 10.30 – 4.30.
Wheelchairs: Good surfaces.
Toilets: Yes. **Dogs:** On lead. **Credit cards:** Yes.

MORDEN HALL PARK (NT)
Open: All year during daylight hours, but car park by the garden centre, café and shop close at 6.

PLANT CENTRE

11/2 THOMMO'S FLOWERS
237 Sutton Common Road,
Sutton, Surrey SM3 9PY
0181 – 641 5226

PICK-YOUR-OWN FARM

11/3 NORTH LOOE FRUIT FARM
Reigate Road,
Ewell, Surrey KT17 3DC
0181 – 393 0256

NURSERIES & GARDEN CENTRES

11/4 BEECHCROFT NURSERY
127 Reigate Road,
Ewell, Surrey KT17 3DE
0181 – 393 4265

A nursery growing conifers, alpines, heathers, perennials and summer and winter bedding plants.
Open: All year EXCEPT Christmas – New Year and August holidays. 7 days a week. Weekdays, summer 10 – 5, winter 10 – 4; Sundays 10 – 4 all year.
Wheelchairs: There is reasonable access.
Toilets: Ask if desperate. **Dogs:** No.
Credit cards: No.

11/5 ROCKHAM NURSERY
139 Reigate Road,
Ewell, Surrey KT17 3DV
0181 – 394 2186

11/6 VERNON GERANIUM NURSERY
Cuddington Way,
Cheam, Surrey
SM2 7JB
0181 – 393 7616

A wide variety of pelargoniums available from the nursery or mail order, plus fuchsias and patio plants.
Open: 1 February – 31 August. 7 days a week, Mondays – Saturdays 9.30 – 5.30, Sundays 10 – 4.
Wheelchairs: Reasonable access to retail area.
Toilets: Yes. **Dogs:** On lead. **Credit cards:** Yes.

11/7 S. G. CLARKE MARKET GARDEN & NURSERY
23 Croydon Lane,
Banstead, Surrey SM7 3BF
0181 – 643 3836
CLOSED CHRISTMAS – MARCH.

Road Atlas for Gardeners

MORDEN – BANSTEAD 11

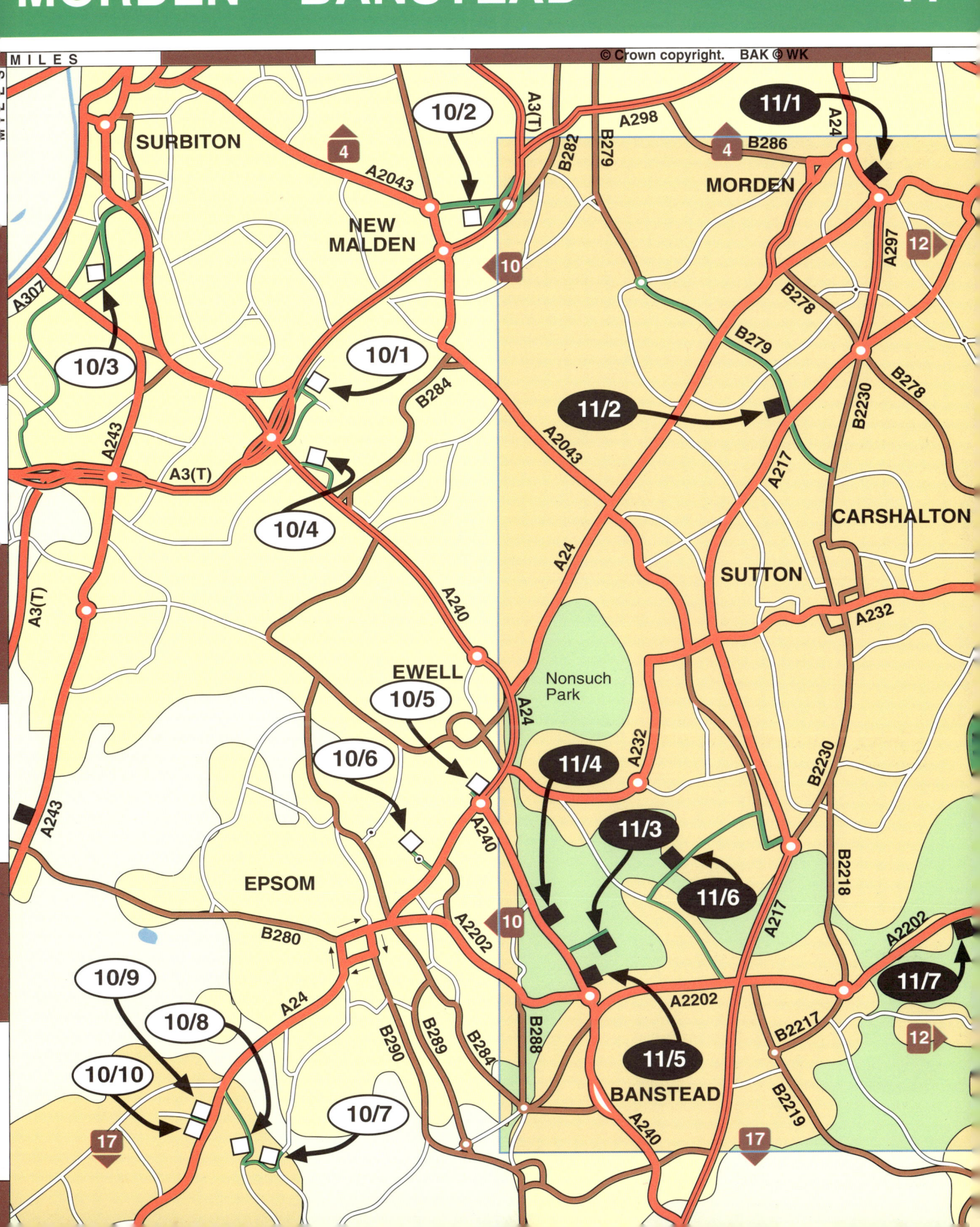

SURREY

NURSERIES & GARDEN CENTRES

12/1 RUSKIN ROAD GARDEN CENTRE
Ruskin Road,
Carshalton, Surrey SM5 3DD
0181 – 669 8205

12/2 MELBOURNE NURSERY
43 Woodmansterne Lane,
Wallington,
Surrey SM6 0SW
0181 – 647 2368

Family nursery growing bedding plants, flowers, pot plants. Also hanging baskets and planted containers.
Open: All year except Christmas Day. 6 days a week (CLOSED MONDAYS but open 7 days a week in the spring bedding season), 9 – 7 when busy.
Wheelchairs: Some concrete, some gravel paths.
Toilets: No.   **Dogs:** On lead.   **Credit cards:** No.

12/3 WOODCOTE GREEN LANE
Woodmansterne Lane,
Wallington, Surrey SM6 0SV
0181 – 647 6838

12/4 BRIAN HILEY
Telegraph Track,
25 Little Woodcote Estate,
Wallington, Surrey SM5 4AU
0181 – 647 9679

Specialist in tender and unusual perennials, penstemons, Salvia canna and ornamental grasses.
Open: Wednesdays – Saturdays 9 – 5.
Wheelchairs: Partial access.
Toilets: Ask if desperate.   **Dogs:** No.
Credit cards: No.

12/5 G. J. BEADLE
53 Woodmansterne Lane,
Wallington, Surrey SM6 05V
0181 – 647 7810

12/6 BARNES NURSERY
46 Woodmansterne Lane,
Wallington, Surrey SM6 0SW
0181 – 647 8213

A long established family nursery. Specialists in summer and winter hanging baskets – new and refill.
Open: All year except Christmas and Boxing Days. 7 days a week, 8.30 – 5.30.
Wheelchairs: The areas are paved.
Toilets: Ask if desperate.   **Dogs:** On lead.
Credit cards: Yes.

12/7 WONDER NURSERIES
69 Lower Pillory Downs,
Little Woodcote,
Carshalton,
Surrey SM5 4DD
0181 – 668 3133

An old established nursery specialising in fuchsias, geraniums, universal pansies and bedding plants.
Open: All year except Christmas week. 7 days a week, 9 – 6 in summer, 9 – 4 in winter (when clocks change).
Wheelchairs: Paved access.
Toilets: Ask if desperate.   **Dogs:** On lead.
Credit cards: No.

12/8 FLITTON'S NURSERY AND PLANT CENTRE
51 Woodmansterne Lane,
Wallington, Surrey SM6 0SW
0181 – 647 5615

An old established family nursery specialising in bedding plants and hanging baskets (also Teleflorist).
Open: 365 days a year, 9 – 5.
Wheelchairs: Easy paved access.
Toilets: No.   **Dogs:** On lead.   **Credit cards:** Yes.

PICK-YOUR-OWN FARM

12/9 SUNRAY FARM
59 Woodmansterne Lane,
Carshalton, Surrey
0181 – 647 7649

Road Atlas for Gardeners

WALLINGTON AREA 12

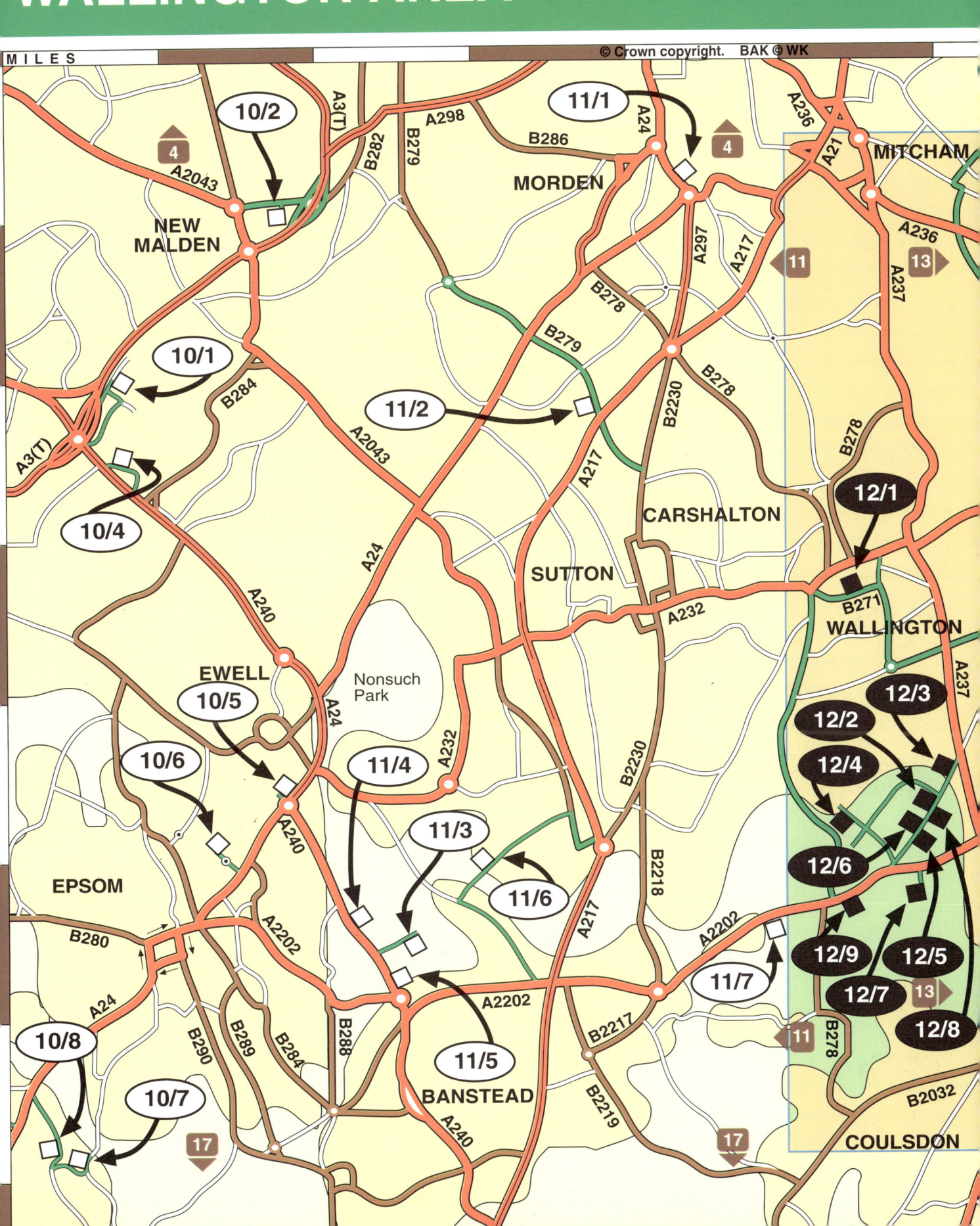

SURREY

NURSERIES & GARDEN CENTRES

13/1 HOMEBASE

13/2 LAWMANS GARDEN CENTRE
28–32 Beddington Lane, Beddington,
Croydon, Surrey CR0 4TC
0181 – 680 0616

13/3 B & Q

13/4 THE GARDEN MARKET
36 Bingham Road,
Addiscombe, Surrey CR0 7EA
0181 – 654 4777

13/5 CROYDON GARDEN CENTRE

13/6 GARDENSTORE AT TEXAS

13/7 COULSDON GARDEN MARKET
185 Brighton Road,
Coulsdon, Surrey
0181 – 763 2802

13/8 KENNEDYS GARDEN CENTRE
Waddon Way, Purley Way,
Croydon, Surrey CR0 4HY
0181 – 688 5117

WATER GARDEN CENTRE

13/9 WORLD OF WATER
Kennedys Garden Centre,
Waddon Way, Purley Way,
Croydon, Surrey CR0 4HY
0181 – 681 3132

Aquatic centre within Kennedys. Specialists in water gardening and tropical fish. Free advice.
Open: All year except Christmas and Boxing Days. 7 days a week, weekdays 9 – 6, Sundays 11 – 5.
Wheelchairs: Reasonable paved access.
Toilets: Yes.   **Dogs:** On lead.   **Credit cards:** Yes.

PICK-YOUR-OWN FARM

13/10 HEATHFIELD FARM PICK-YOUR-OWN
Gravel Hill (A212), Selsdon,
South Croydon, Surrey
0181 – 657 7890

Pick-your-own fruit and veg: strawberries, raspberries, plums, apples, asparagus, rhubarb, runner beans and more!
Open: May – October. 7 days a week,
May – August 9 – 7, September and October 9 – 6.
Wheelchairs: Yes.
Toilets: No.   **Dogs:** No.   **Credit cards:** No.

GARDEN & NURSERY

13/11 COOMBE WOOD GARDENS AND NURSERY

Open: Garden: all year except Christmas Day, dawn – dusk.
Nursery: Tuesdays, Wednesdays and Thursdays only, 2 – 4.

GARDEN

13/12 HEATHFIELD

Open: All year except Christmas Day; 7 days a week, dawn – dusk.
Costs: Free.

Road Atlas for Gardeners

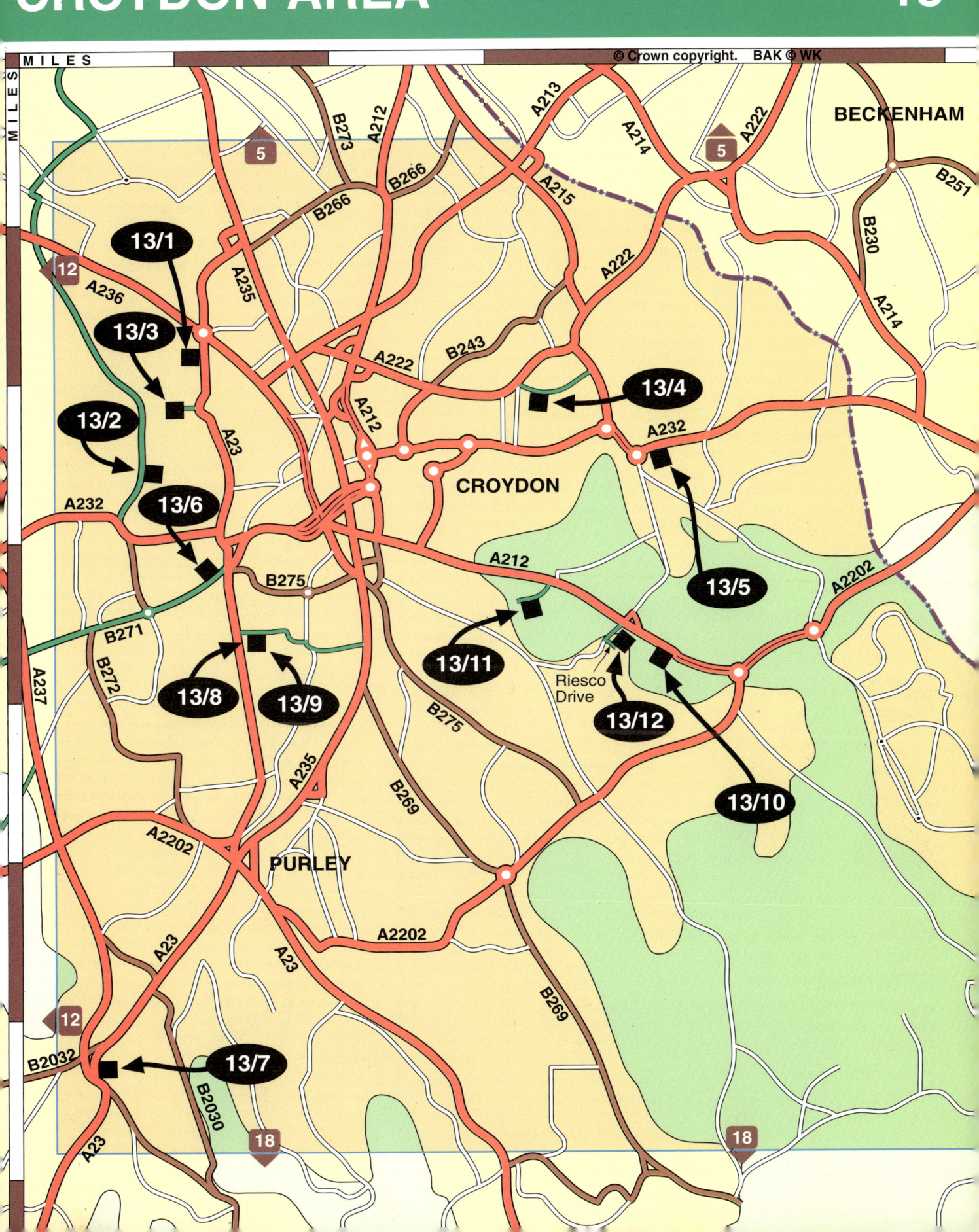

CROYDON AREA 13

SURREY

NURSERIES & GARDEN CENTRES

14/1 HOMEBASE

14/2 MERRIST WOOD PLANT CENTRE
Merrist Wood College, Holly Lane,
Worplesdon,
Guildford, Surrey GU3 3PE
01483 – 232 424
A wide range of trees, shrubs, conifers, perennials, alpines, bedding and house plants.
Open: All year. Mondays – Fridays, 9 – 5, weekends, SPRING & SUMMER ONLY (& other selected weekends – phone for dates), 10.30 – 5.30.
Wheelchairs: Hard surfaces, no steps.
Toilets: Yes.   **Dogs:** On lead.   **Credit cards:** No.

14/3 BLACKHORSE PLANTS
Blackhorse Road,
Woking, Surrey GU22 0QS
0483 – 797 534

14/4 THE OLD GARDENS
Blackhorse Road,
Woking, Surrey GU22 0QS
01483 – 473 278

14/5 JOHN GUNNER GARDEN CENTRE
Sunnyside, Clasford Bridge,
Aldershot Road, Worplesdon,
Guildford, Surrey GU3 3RE
01483 – 233 543
Old established family garden centre specialising in hard landscaping materials and all plant needs.
Open: All year except Christmas – New Year. Mondays – Saturdays 8 – 5, Sundays 10 – 4.
Wheelchairs: Easy paved access with ramps.
Toilets: No.   **Dogs:** No.   **Credit cards:** Yes.

14/6 BARRALETS NURSERY AND GARDEN CENTRE
Guildford Road, Pirbright,
Woking, Surrey GU24 0LM
0483 – 476 154

14/7 TANGLEY GARDENS NURSERY
Pitch Place, Worplesdon Road,
Guildford, Surrey GU3 3LQ
01483 – 232 243
Open: Mondays – Fridays 9 – 5.30.

14/8 WOODLANDS FARM NURSERY
Woodstreet Village,
Guildford, Surrey GU3 3DU
01483 – 235 536
Secondhand and antique garden ornaments and reclaimed materials, mature conifers, trees, shrubs and hedging.
Open: By appointment only.

SEE PAGE 43 FOR FULL DETAILS

14/9 THE GLEN AND NURSERY
13 Nutshell Lane, Upper Hale,
Farnham, Surrey GU9 0HC
01252 – 724 963

PICK-YOUR-OWN FARM

14/10 MANOR FARM
Tongham,
Farnham, Surrey GU10 1DC
01252 – 782 680

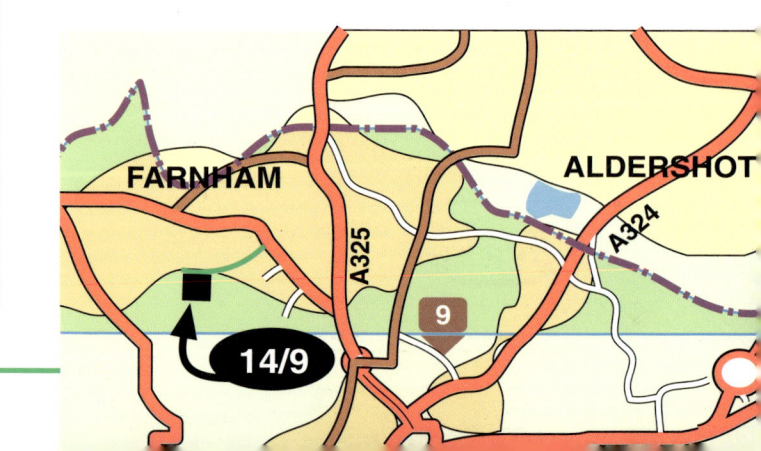

Road Atlas for Gardeners

NORTH WEST OF GUILDFORD　　14

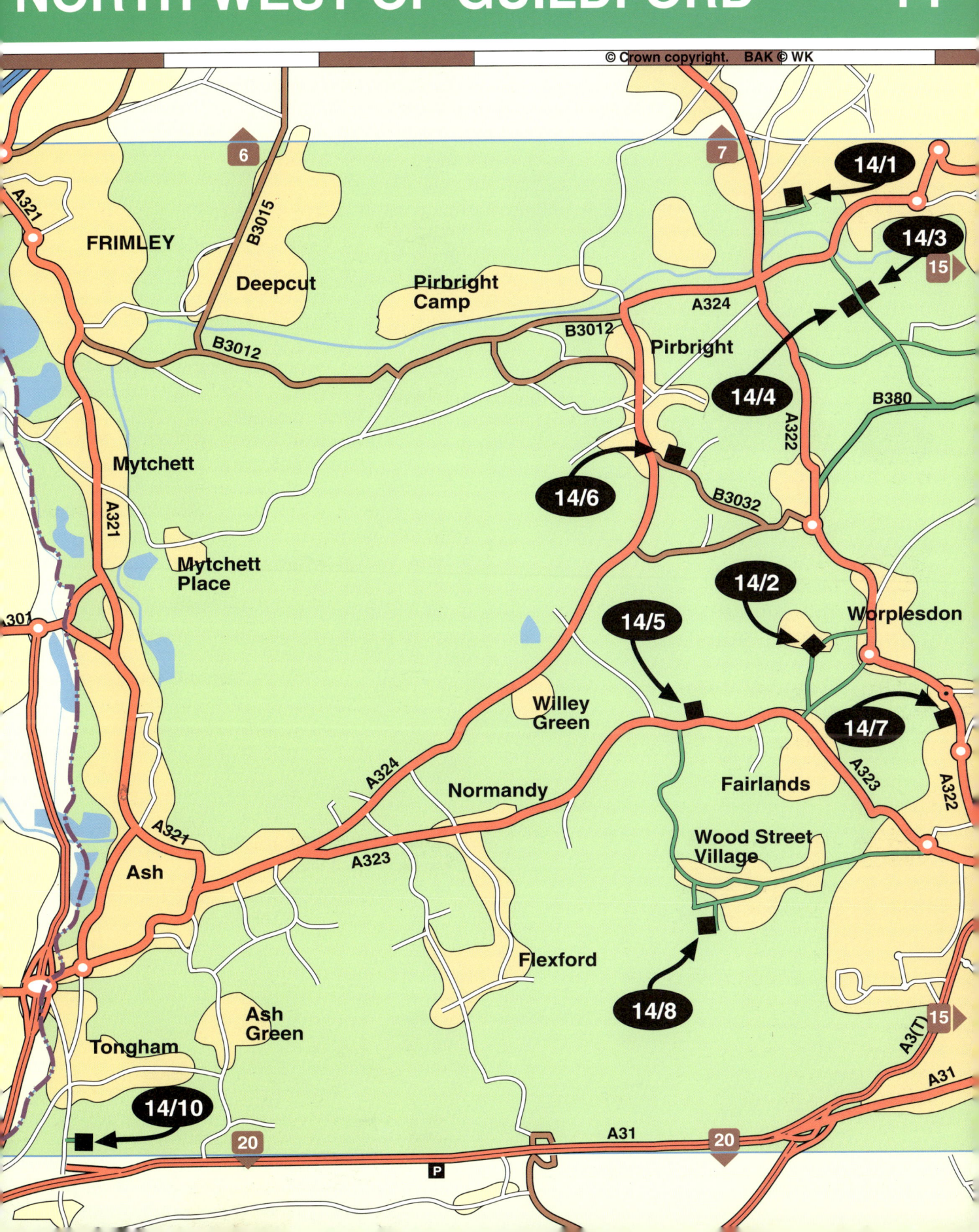

SURREY

NURSERIES & GARDEN CENTRES

15/1 BRIARWOOD NURSERY & GARDEN CENTRE
Saunders Lane,
Mayford,
Woking, Surrey
GU22 0NT
01483 – 763 216

An old established family-run nursery with a wide variety of stock, unusual shrubs and herbaceous plants.
Open: All year except Christmas Day and the week after. 7 days a week, weekdays 9 – 5, Sundays 10 – 4.
Wheelchairs: Easy paved access without steps.
Toilets: Yes.   **Dogs:** On lead.   **Credit cards:** Yes.

15/2 JACKMAN'S GARDEN CENTRE
Egley Road, Mayford,
Woking, Surrey GU22 0NH
01483 – 714 861

15/3 ELM NURSERY
Sutton Green Road,
Guildford, Surrey GU4 7QE
01483 – 761 748

15/4 RIPLEY NURSERIES
Portsmouth Road, Ripley,
Woking, Surrey GU23 6EV
01483 – 225 090

15/5 B & Q

15/6 HOMEBASE

GARDEN CENTRE & PYO FARM

15/7 SUTTON GREEN GARDEN NURSERY
Guildford Road, Sutton Green,
Guildford, Surrey, GU4 7QA
01483 – 232 366

Seasonal bedding plants, shrubs, trees, herbaceous and alpines. PYO strawberries, raspberries and other fruit.
Open: All year except Christmas, Boxing and New Year's Days. Mondays – Saturdays 8.30 – 5.30; Sunday 9.30 – 5.30.
Wheelchairs: Paved access.
Toilets: Ask if desperate.   **Dogs:** Yes, except in PYO fields.   **Credit cards:** Yes.

PICK-YOUR-OWN FARMS

15/8 NUTBERRY FRUIT FARM
Portsmouth Road, Ripley, Surrey

15/9 NUTHILL FRUIT FARM
Open: For soft fruit, mid June – end July.

GARDEN & GARDEN CENTRE

15/10 CLANDON PARK (NT)
Open: Weekends only in March, then 1 April – 29 October daily (EXCEPT THURSDAYS & FRIDAYS but open Good Friday), 1.30 – 5.30.
Costs: Adults, £4.00 including house and museum.

15/11 CLANDON PARK GARDEN CENTRE
West Clandon,
Guildford,
Surrey GU4 7RQ
01483 – 222 925

A garden centre specialising in unusual plants, trees, shrubs; extensive range of roses and herbaceous plants.
Open: All year except Christmas and Boxing Days. 7 days a week, summer 8.30 – 6, winter (with clock change) 9 – 5.
Wheelchairs: Gravelled car park and paths.
Toilets: Yes.   **Dogs:** On lead.   **Credit cards:** Yes.

GARDENS

15/12 ROYAL HORTICULTURAL SOCIETY GARDEN, WISLEY
Woking, Surrey GU23 6QB
01483 – 224 234

The Royal Horticultural Society's 240-acre gardens. Gardeners' bookshop, plant centre.
Open: All year except Christmas Day. Mondays – Saturdays (MEMBERS ONLY ON SUNDAYS), 10 – sunset or 7 in summer.
Costs: Adults, £4.70; children, £1.75.
Wheelchairs: Good access. Wheelchairs available.

15/13 HATCHLANDS PARK (NT)
Open: 2 April – end October: Tuesdays, Wednesdays, Thursdays, Sundays and Bank Holiday Mondays only (and Fridays in August), 2 – 5.30.
Costs: Garden free.   **Wheelchairs:** Access to part of garden. There are disabled toilets.

Road Atlas for Gardeners

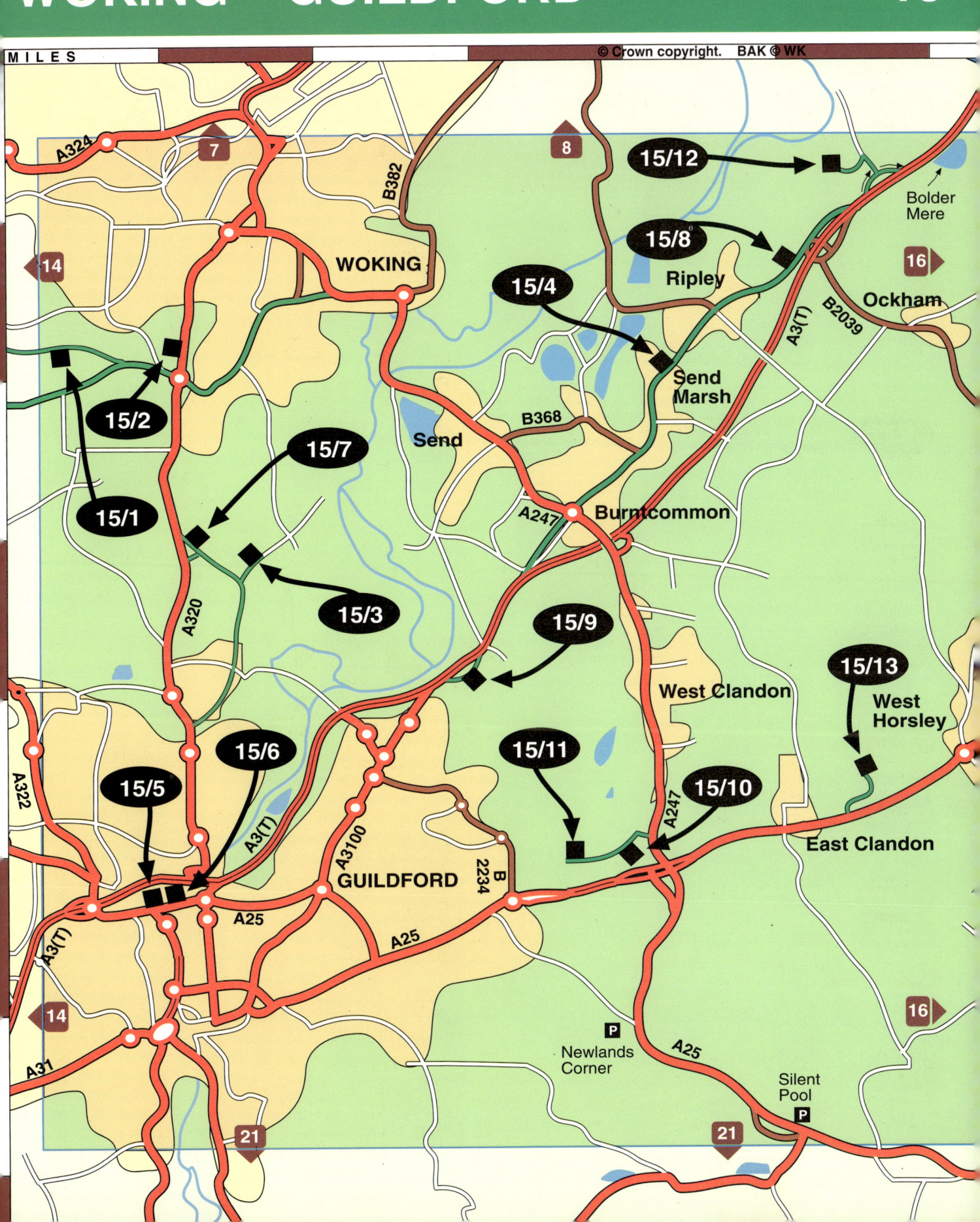

WOKING – GUILDFORD   15

SURREY

NURSERIES & GARDEN CENTRES

16/1 B & Q

16/2 **CEDAR NURSERY**
Horsley Road,
Cobham, Surrey GU10 1PL
01932 – 862 473
A country nursery growing a wide range of trees and shrubs. Specialists in garden design.
Open: All year except Christmas, Boxing and New Year's Days. 7 days a week, Mondays – Fridays 8 – 5, Saturdays and Sundays 10 – 5.
Toilets: Ask if desperate.   **Dogs:** On lead.
Credit cards: Yes.

16/3 **LOWER ROAD PLANT CENTRE**
Lower Road,
Effingham,
Leatherhead,
Surrey
KT24 5JP

Specialities are clematis, hanging baskets and hardy nursery stock. Friendly staff!
Open: All year except Christmas and Boxing Days. Mondays – Saturdays 9 – 5, Sundays 10 – 4.
Wheelchairs: The area is paved and aisles are wide enough for access.
Toilets: Ask if desperate.   **Dogs:** On lead.
Credit cards: Yes.

16/4 **DOBBE'S NURSERIES**
Guildford Road,
Great Bookham, Surrey KT23 4EY
01372 – 454 553

16/5 **WEST HORSLEY GARDEN CENTRE**
Epsom Road,
West Horsley, Surrey KT24 6AP
01483 – 282 911

16/6 **CROCKNORTH NURSERY**
Crocknorth Road, East Horsley,
Leatherhead, Surrey KT24 5TC
01483 – 285 376

16/7 **HERBS AND SCENTED PLANTS**
Crocknorth Road, Ranmore,
Dorking, Surrey RH5 6SY
01486 – 282 273

VINEYARD

16/8 **DENBIES WINE ESTATE**
London Road,
Dorking, Surrey RH5 6AA
01306 – 876 616

GARDEN

16/9 **POLESDEN LACEY (NT)**
Great Bookham,
Near Dorking,
Surrey RH5 6BD
01372 – 452 048
Almost 1200 acres of formal gardens, beautiful parkland, woods, estate walks and exceptional views. Plant sales area.
Open: Gardens and grounds all year. 7 days a week, 11 – 6 or dusk if earlier.
Costs: Adults, £2.50.
Wheelchairs: Access to parts of garden, showroom and restaurant. Self-drive buggy available by arrangement. Braille guide. There are disabled toilets.
Toilets: Yes.
Dogs: Not in formal gardens; on lead in grounds.

Road Atlas for Gardeners

LEATHERHEAD – DORKING 16

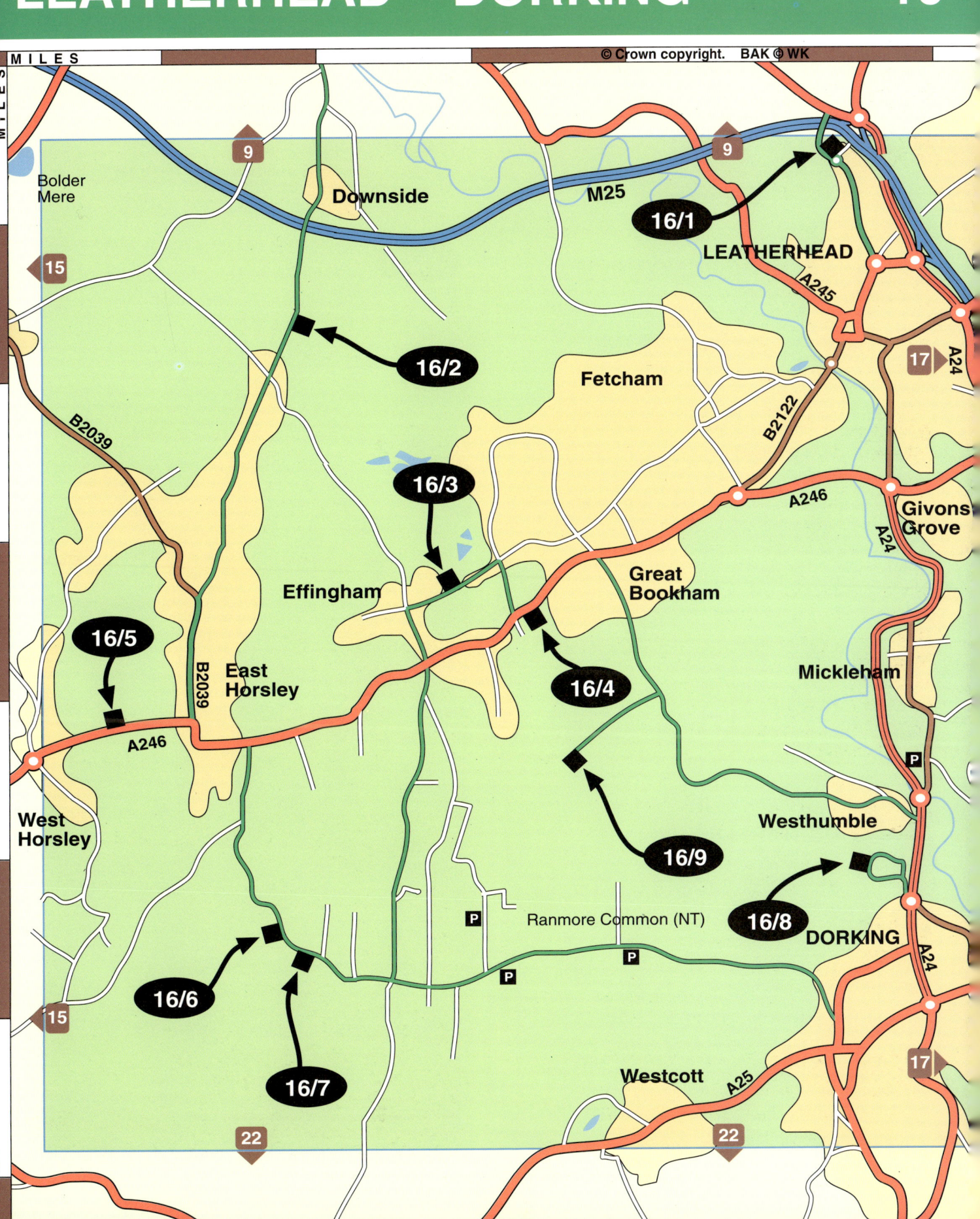

SURREY

NURSERIES & GARDEN CENTRES

17/1 **FANNY'S FARM SHOP**
Markedge Lane,
Merstham, Surrey RH1 3AM
01737 – 554 444

17/2 **THE MICHAEL SEYMOUR NURSERY**
Station Road,
Betchworth, Surrey RH3 7LX
01737 – 842 099
Hardy nursery stock, shrubs, roses, herbaceous plants, bedding plants, ornamental and fruit trees, conifers, sundries.
Open: All year except Christmas – New Year's Day inclusive. 7 days a week, Mondays – Saturdays 8 – 5.30 or dusk if earlier (but extended hours in spring and early summer), Sundays 10 – 4.
Wheelchairs: Display areas are paved.
Toilets: Yes.   **Dogs:** On lead.   **Credit cards:** Yes.

17/3 **COUNTRY GARDEN CENTRE**

17/4 **BUCKLAND NURSERIES**
A25, Buckland,
Near Reigate, Surrey RH2 9RF
01737 – 242 990

17/5 **HIGH TREES NURSERIES**
Buckland,
Near Reigate, Surrey RH2 9RF
01737 – 247 217

17/6 **WHEELERS LANE NURSERY**
Wheelers Lane, Brockham,
Betchworth, Surrey RH3 7HS
01737 – 844 575

17/7 **HEATHFIELD NURSERIES**
Flanchford Road,
Reigate Heath, Surrey RH2 8AA
01737 – 247 641

17/8 **REIGATE GARDEN CENTRE**
143 Sandcross Lane, South Park,
Reigate, Surrey RH2 8HH
01737 – 248 188

Gillian Cutress

Road Atlas for Gardeners

WEST OF REIGATE
17

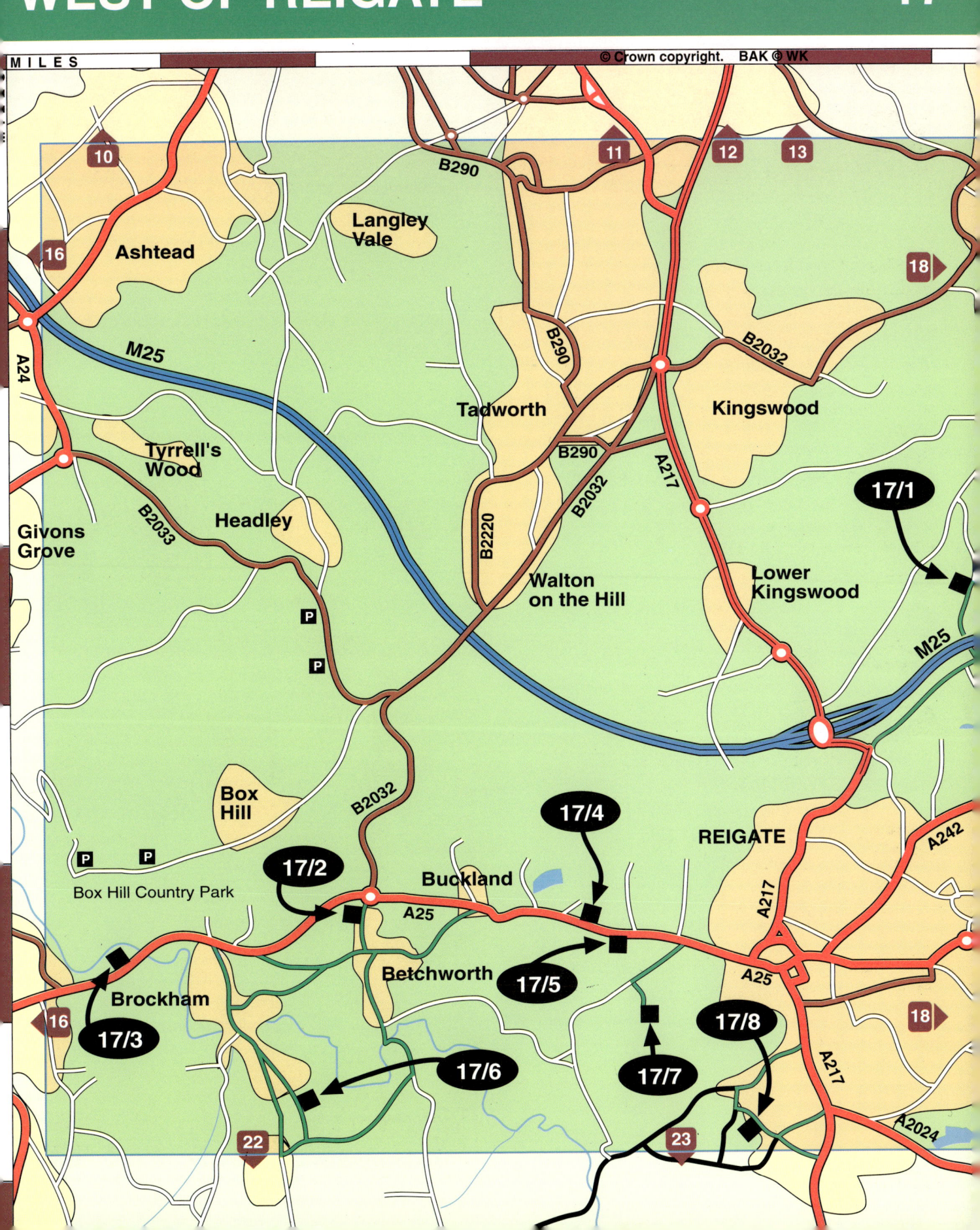

SURREY

VINEYARD

18/1 GODSTONE VINEYARDS
Quarry Road,
Godstone, Surrey RH9 8ZA
01883 – 744 590
Vineyard with self- and group-guided tours; gift shop; adopt-a-vine; light lunches all day.
Open: All year except Christmas and Boxing Days. 7 days a week, 10 – 5.30.
Wheelchairs: Yes.
Toilets: Yes.   **Dogs:** On lead.   **Credit cards:** Yes.

NURSERIES & GARDEN CENTRES

18/2 KNIGHTS GARDEN CENTRE
Chelsham Place, Limpsfield Road,
Chelsham, Surrey CR6 9DZ
01883 – 622 340

18/3 KNIGHTS GARDEN CENTRE
Rosedene Nursery,
Woldingham, Surrey CR3 7LA
01883 – 653 142

18/4 CLAY LANE NURSERY
THE SURREY FUCHSIA CENTRE,
3 Clay Lane, South Nutfield,
Redhill, Surrey RH1 4EG
01737 – 823 307
A specialist fuchsia nursery. Rooted cuttings for sale February – mid April, mature plants May – August.
Open: 28 Jan – 31 March: 6 days a week (CLOSED MONDAYS except Easter), 9 – 5. 1 April – 30 June: 7 days a week, 9 – 5. 1 July – 31 Aug: 7 days a week, 9 – 5, BUT PHONE FIRST TO CHECK.
Toilets: Ask if desperate. **Dogs:** No. **Credit cards:** No.

18/5 IVY MILL NURSERY
Bletchingly Road,
Godstone, Surrey RH9 8DA
01883 – 742 665

18/6 NETTLETON'S NURSERY
Ivy Mill Lane,
Godstone, Surrey RH9 8NE
01883 – 742 426

18/7 KNIGHTS GARDEN CENTRE
Nag's Hall Nursery,
Godstone, Surrey RH9 8DA
01883 – 742 275

PLANT CENTRE & PICK-YOUR-OWN FARM

18/8 PRIORY FARM
Nutfield, Redhill,
Surrey
RH1 4EJ
PYO: 01737 – 822 484
Plant centre: 01737 – 823 500
Specialist growers of bedding plants and hanging baskets, with good range of potted plants and perennials. Also pick-your-own, farm shop and coffee shop.
Wheelchairs: Easy access.
Toilets: Yes.   **Dogs:** Only in car parks.
Credit cards: Yes (except PYO).

SEE PAGE 43 FOR FULL DETAILS OF OPENING DATES AND TIMES.

PICK-YOUR-OWN FARM

18/9 FLOWER FARM
The Oxted Road (A25),
Godstone, Surrey RH9 8ZA
01883 – 743 636 (24 hours)
PYO fruit & vegetables; strawberries, raspberries, plums, apples, asparagus, rhubarb, runner beans and more!
Open: May – October, 7 days a week. May – August 9 – 7, September and October 9 – 6.
Wheelchairs: Yes.
Toilets: No.   **Dogs:** No.   **Credit cards:** No.

Road Atlas for Gardeners

REDHILL – GODSTONE   18

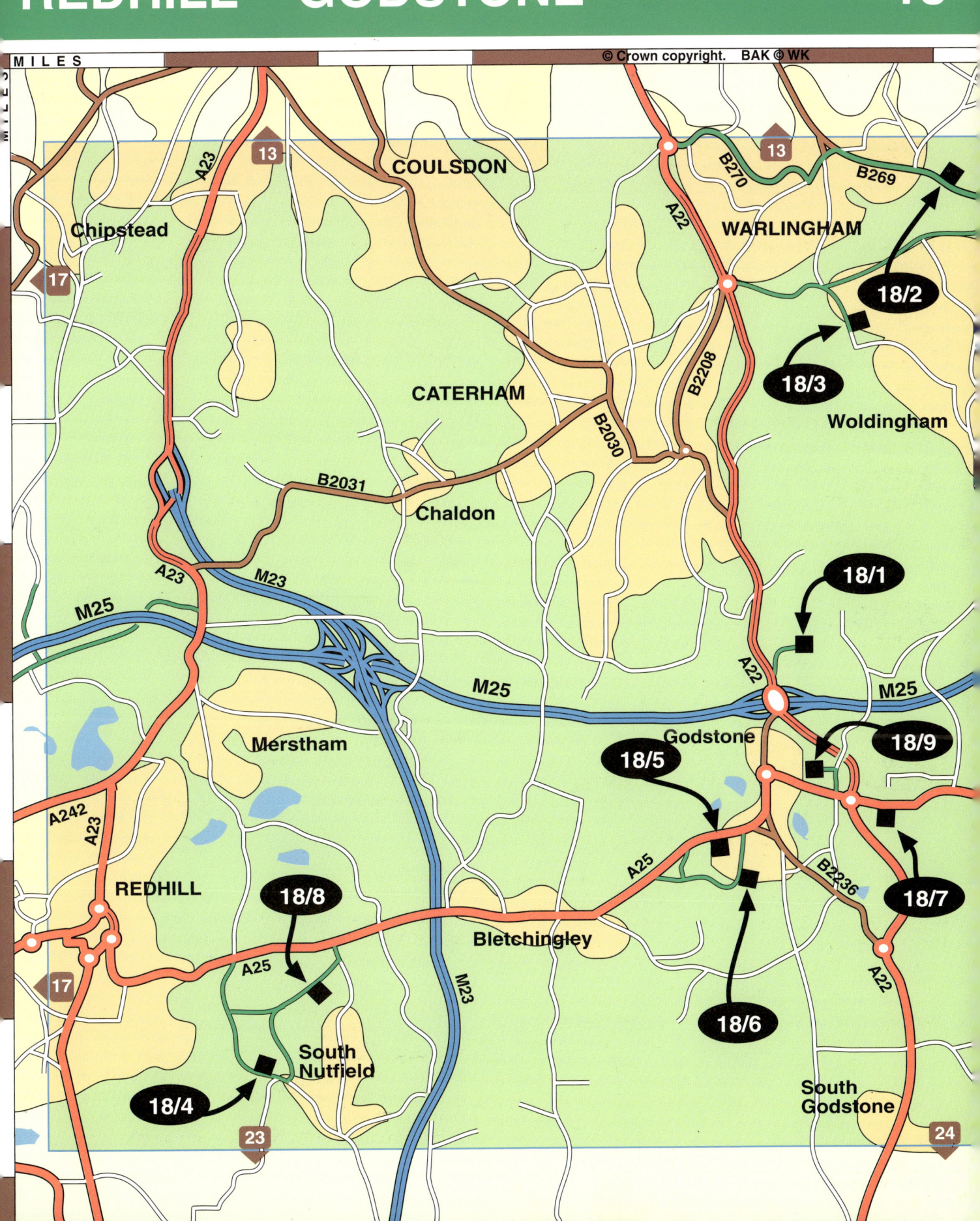

SURREY

NURSERIES & GARDEN CENTRES

19/1 MONKTON NURSERIES
Lower Monkton Lane,
Farnham, Surrey GU9 9ND
01252 – 711 268

19/2 BADSHOT LEA GARDEN CENTRE
Badshot Lea,
Farnham, Surrey GU9 9JJ
0252 – 333 666

19/3 LITTLE ACRES NURSERY
St. Georges Road, Badshot Lea, Runfold,
Farnham, Surrey GU10 1PR
01252 – 782 942

19/4 BOURNE MILL GARDEN CENTRE
Guildford Road,
Farnham, Surrey GU9 9QA
0252 – 734 293

19/5 FRENSHAM GARDEN CENTRE
The Reeds,
Frensham,
Surrey
GU10 3BP
01252 – 792 545

A garden centre set in mature woodland with a wide range of trees, shrubs and plants. Coffee and craft shop.
Open: All year except Christmas and Boxing Days. 7 days a week, Monday – Saturday 9 – 5.30; Sundays 10.30 – 4.30.
Wheelchairs: Easy level access.
Toilets: Yes.   **Dogs:** On lead.   **Credit cards:** Yes.

19/6 GARDEN STYLE
Wrecclesham Hill,
Farnham, Surrey GU10 4JY
01252 – 735 331

19/7 MILLAIS NURSERIES
Crosswater Lane, Churt,
Farnham, Surrey GU10 2JN
01252 – 792 698

Specialist rhododendron growers with over 600 varieties. 10-acre display garden open in May (£1.50).
Open: All year. Tuesday – Friday 10 – 1 and 2 – 5; Saturdays in March, April, October and November; daily in May.
Wheelchairs: Good paved access.
Toilets: Yes.   **Dogs:** No.   **Credit cards:** Yes.

PICK-YOUR-OWN FARM

19/8 AVALON NURSERIES
Tilford Road, Churt,
Farnham, Surrey GU10 2LL
01428 – 604 842

GARDEN

19/9 BIRDWORLD
Holt Pound,
Farnham,
Surrey
GU10 4LD
01420 – 22140

Hundreds of exotic birds living in 25 acres of parkland and gardens. Bird demonstrations in theatre. Café.
Open: All year except Christmas Day.
March 9.30 – 5; April – August 9.30 – 6;
September 9.30 – 5.30; October 9.30 – 5;
November – February 9.30 – 4.
Costs: Adults, £3.95; children, £2.25; senior citizens, £3.15; family ticket (2 + 2), £11.50.
Wheelchairs: Yes – good paths around gardens.
Toilets: Yes.   **Dogs:** No, except guide dogs.
Credit cards: Not at entrance, but accepted in shop and café.

Road Atlas for Gardeners

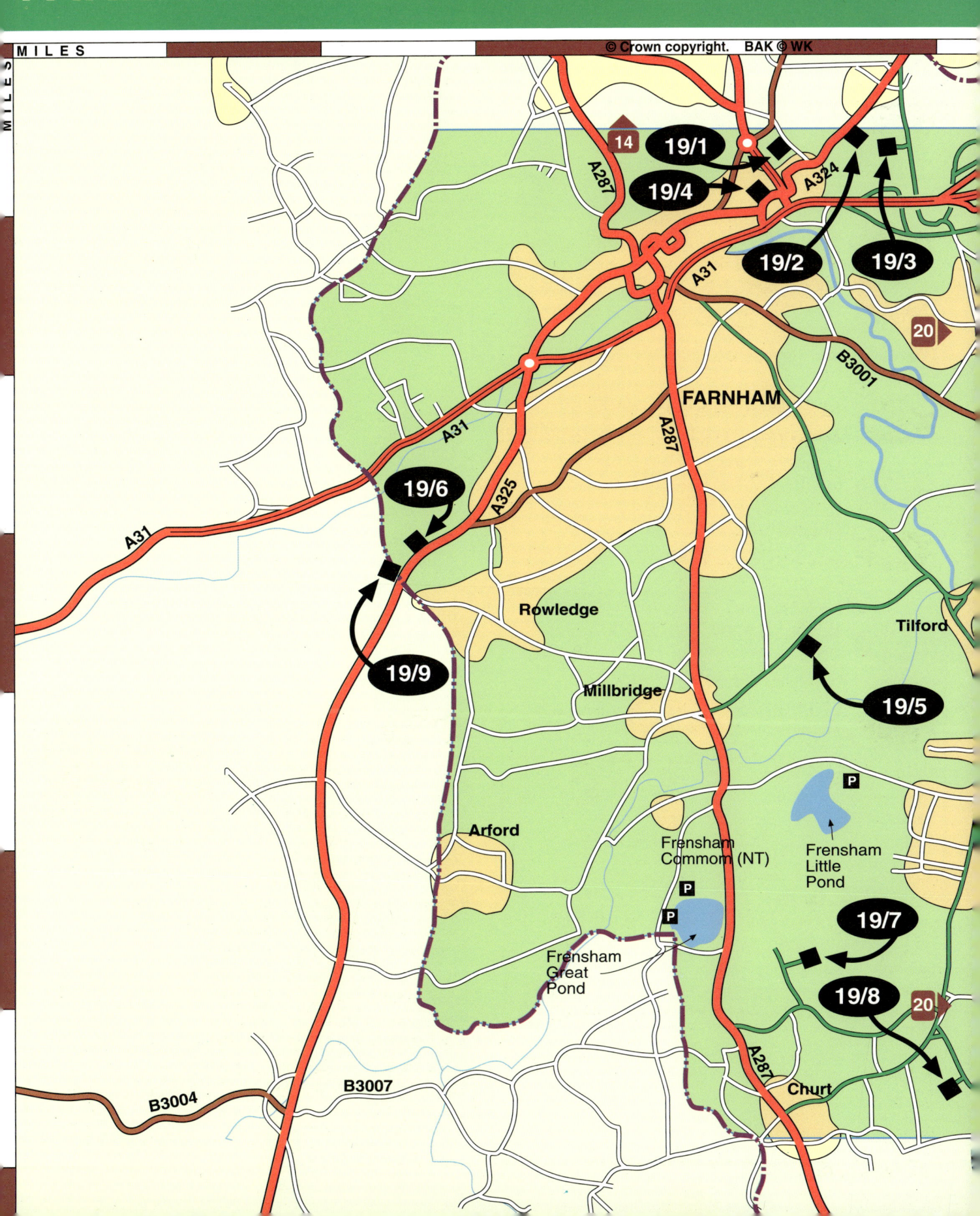

FARNHAM AREA   19

SURREY

NURSERIES & GARDEN CENTRES

20/1 OAK LODGE NURSERIES
Seale Lane,
Seale,
Farnham,
Surrey
GU10 1LD
01252 – 782 410

An old established family nursery with a shrubbery walk and a wide and unusual variety of home-grown plants.
Open: All year except the week following Christmas. 7 days a week, 9 – 5.
Wheelchairs: Gravelled car park but easy access elsewhere.
Toilets: Yes.   **Dogs:** No.   **Credit cards:** Yes.

20/2 COMPTON NURSERY
Compton,
Guildford, Surrey GU3 1DT
01483 – 811 387

20/3 HAZELBANK NURSERY
Tilford Street, Tilford,
Farnham, Surrey GU10 2BN
01252 – 782 405

A nursery growing a complete range of bedding plants, perennials, shrubs and cut flowers.
Open: All year except Christmas week.
7 days a week, summer 9 – 6, winter 9 – dusk; Sundays 10 – 5 all year.
Toilets: No.   **Dogs:** No.   **Credit cards:** Yes.

20/4 WHEELER STREET NURSERY
Wheeler Lane, Witley,
Godalming, Surrey GU8 5QR
01428 – 682 638

PICK-YOUR-OWN FARM

20/5 HYDE ORCHARDS
Hyde Lane, Churt,
Farnham, Surrey
01428 – 604 537

GARDEN CENTRE & PICK-YOUR-OWN FARM

20/6 SECRETTS GARDEN CENTRE AND PICK-YOUR-OWN
Old Portsmouth Road, Milford,
Godalming, Surrey, GU8 5HL
Garden centre 01483 – 426 633
PYO 01483 – 426 543

A large garden centre with a wide range of house, conservatory & garden plants. Also farm & flower shop.
Open: 7 days a week. Mondays – Fridays 9 – 5.30, Saturdays 9.30 – 5.30, Sundays 10 – 4.
Wheelchairs: Accessible.
Toilets: Yes.   **Dogs:** No.   **Credit cards:** Yes.

Road Atlas for Gardeners

WEST OF GODALMING   20

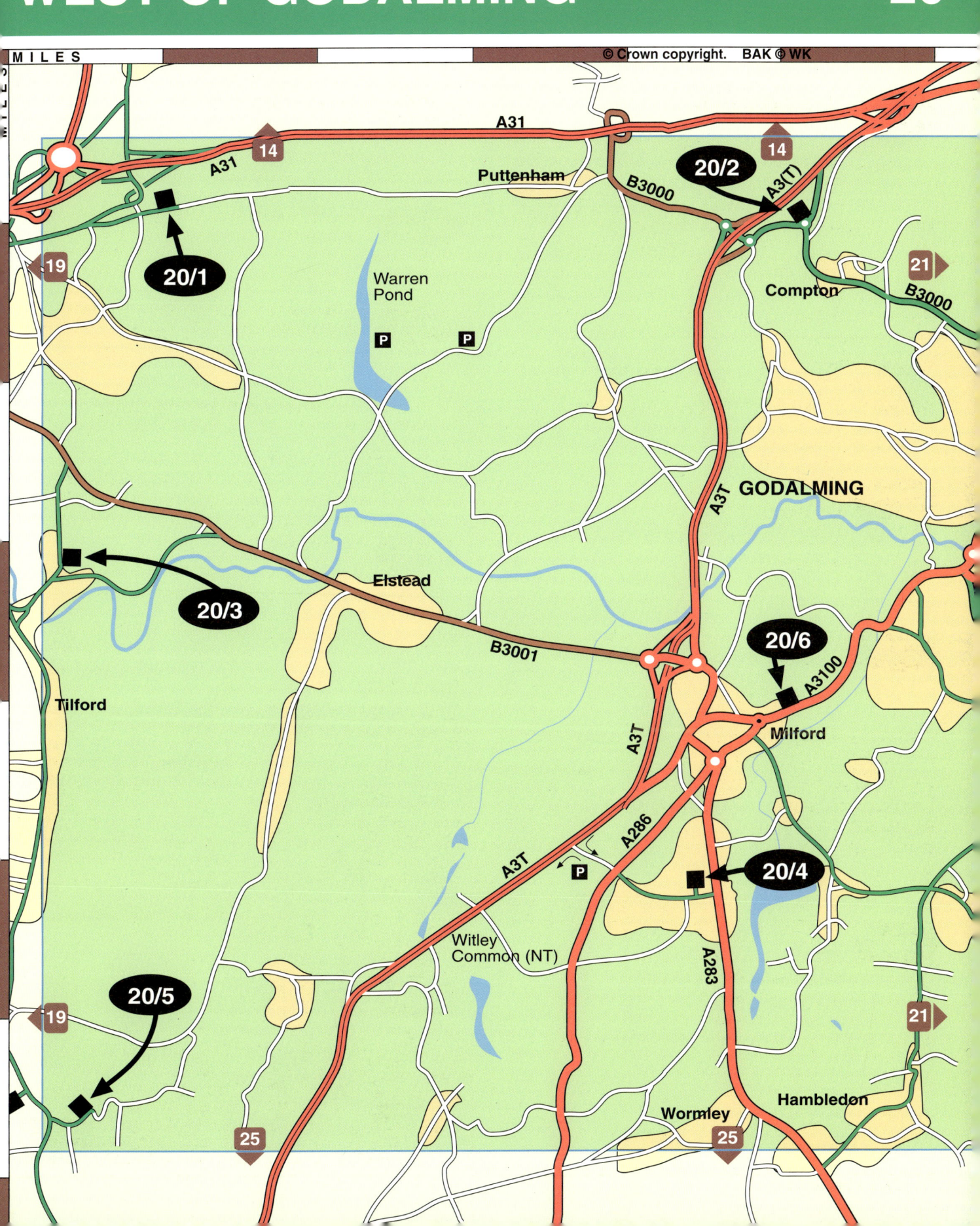

SURREY

NURSERIES & GARDEN CENTRES

21/1 K. DEMETRIADI
Heathfield, Heath Lane, Albury Heath,
Near Guildford, Surrey GU5 9DD
01483 – 202 139
A specialist grower of dwarf rhododendrons and hardy evergreen azaleas – over 50 varieties.
Open: 7 days a week but BY APPOINTMENT ONLY – please telephone first.
Toilets: Yes. **Dogs:** On lead. **Credit cards:** No.

21/2 HEATH NURSERY (LEYLANDII)
Heath Lane, Albury Heath,
Albury, Surrey GU5 9DD
01483 – 203 264

21/3 ASTOLAT
6 Acre Works, Old Portsmouth Road,
Peasmarsh,
Guildford, Surrey GU3 1NF
01483 – 575 213

21/4 HIGHBANKS NURSERY
Birtley Road, Bramley,
Guildford, Surrey GU5 0LB
01483 – 893 380

21/5 HYDON NURSERIES
Clock Barn Lane, Hydon Heath,
Godalming, Surrey GU8 4AZ
01483 – 860 252
A well known nursery with many awards including five Gold Medals at Chelsea Flower Shows.
Open: All year except Christmas.
Wheelchairs: Difficult if unaccompanied.
Toilets: No. **Dogs:** On lead. **Credit cards:** No.

SEE PAGE 43 FOR FULL DETAILS

21/6 NOTCUTTS GARDEN CENTRE
Guildford Road,
Cranleigh, Surrey GU6 8LT
01483 – 274 222

21/7 HOMELEIGH NURSERY
Coombe Lea, Guildford Road,
Cranleigh,
Surrey GU6 8PP
01483 – 274 182
Cut flowers: alstroemerias (many colours), chrysanthemums, carnations – spray and bloom varieties.
Open: Summer and winter; 7 days a week, 9 – dusk.
Wheelchairs: Easy access to packing sheds.
Toilets: Ask if desperate. **Dogs:** On lead.
Credit cards: No.

GARDENS

21/8 LOSELEY PARK FARM
Guildford,
Surrey GU3 1HS
01483 – 304 440
Elizabethan country house lived in since 1562 by the same family. New, formal gardens of flowers & vegetables.
Open: 3 May – 30 September;
Wednesdays – Saturdays (and Bank Holidays), 11 – 5.
Costs: Adults, £1.50; children, 50p.
Wheelchairs: Can tour the gardens.
Toilets: Yes. **Dogs:** Only in field; must be on lead.
Credit cards: No.

21/9 BUSBRIDGE LAKES
Open 22 days a year: for dates telephone
01483 – 421 955

21/10 WINKWORTH ARBORETUM (NT)

Open: All year, 7 days a week during daylight hours.
Costs: Adults, £2.00; children (5 – 17), £1.00.
Wheelchairs: Limited access.

Road Atlas for Gardeners

GODALMING – CRANLEIGH   21

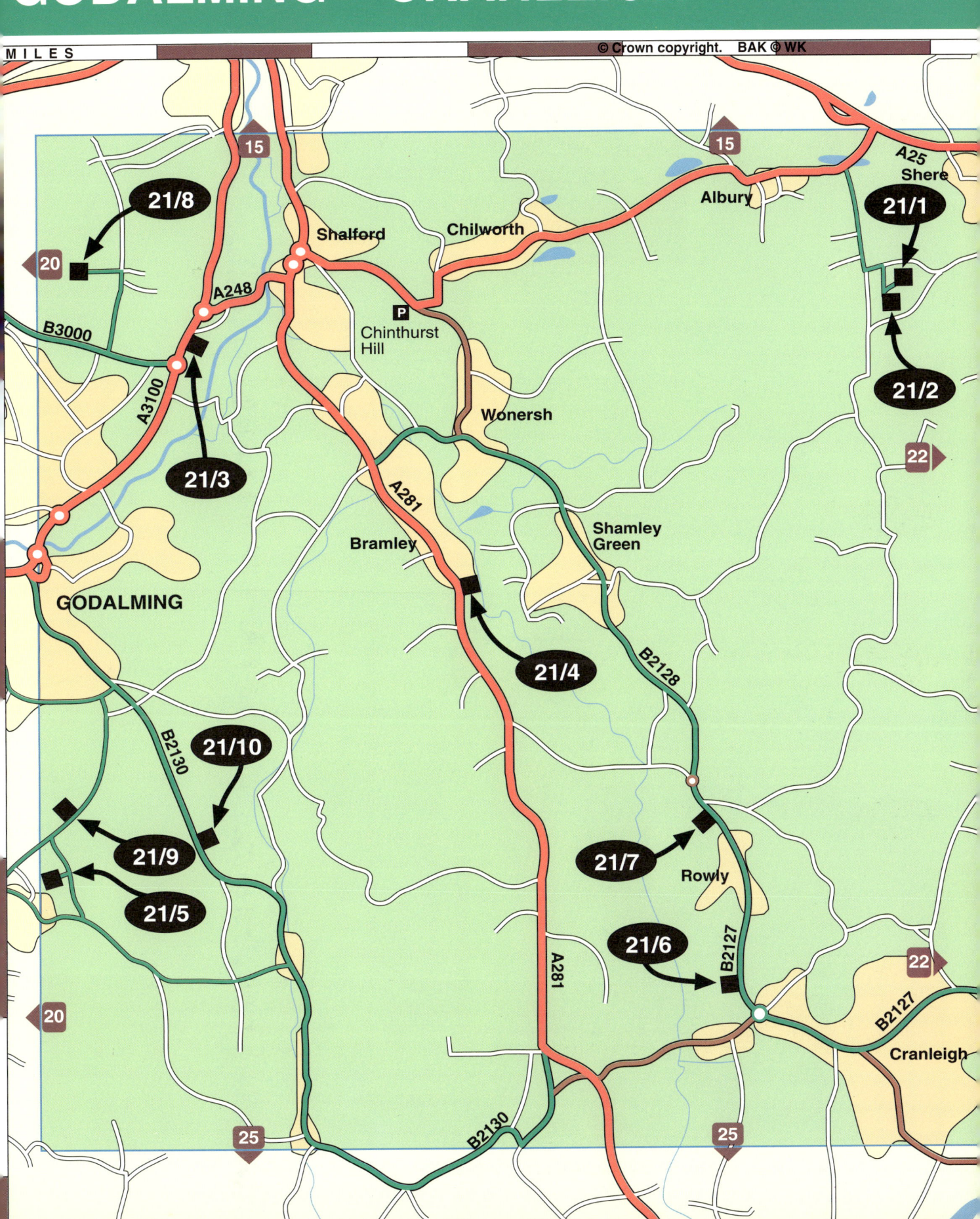

Surrey

PICK-YOUR-OWN FARM

22/1 OCKLEY COURT FARM

Ockley,
Near Dorking,
Surrey
RH5 5LS
01306 – 711 365

Farm shop with freshest home grown fruit, vegetables, salads. Plants, hanging baskets. PYO soft fruit, vegetables.
Open: Farm shop all year. 7 days a week, summer 9–6, winter 9–5.
PYO June–August, 9–7; September 9–6.
Wheelchairs: Not suitable.
Toilets: Yes.   **Dogs:** On lead.
Credit cards: Yes, in shop, but not in PYO.

GARDENS

22/2 HANNAH PESCHAR SCULPTURE GARDEN

Open: 2nd Sunday in May – 31 October. Fridays & Saturdays 11 – 6, Sundays & Bank Holidays 2 – 5.
Costs: Adults, £4.00; children, £2.00; OAPs, £3.00.

Paul Temple

Road Atlas for Gardeners

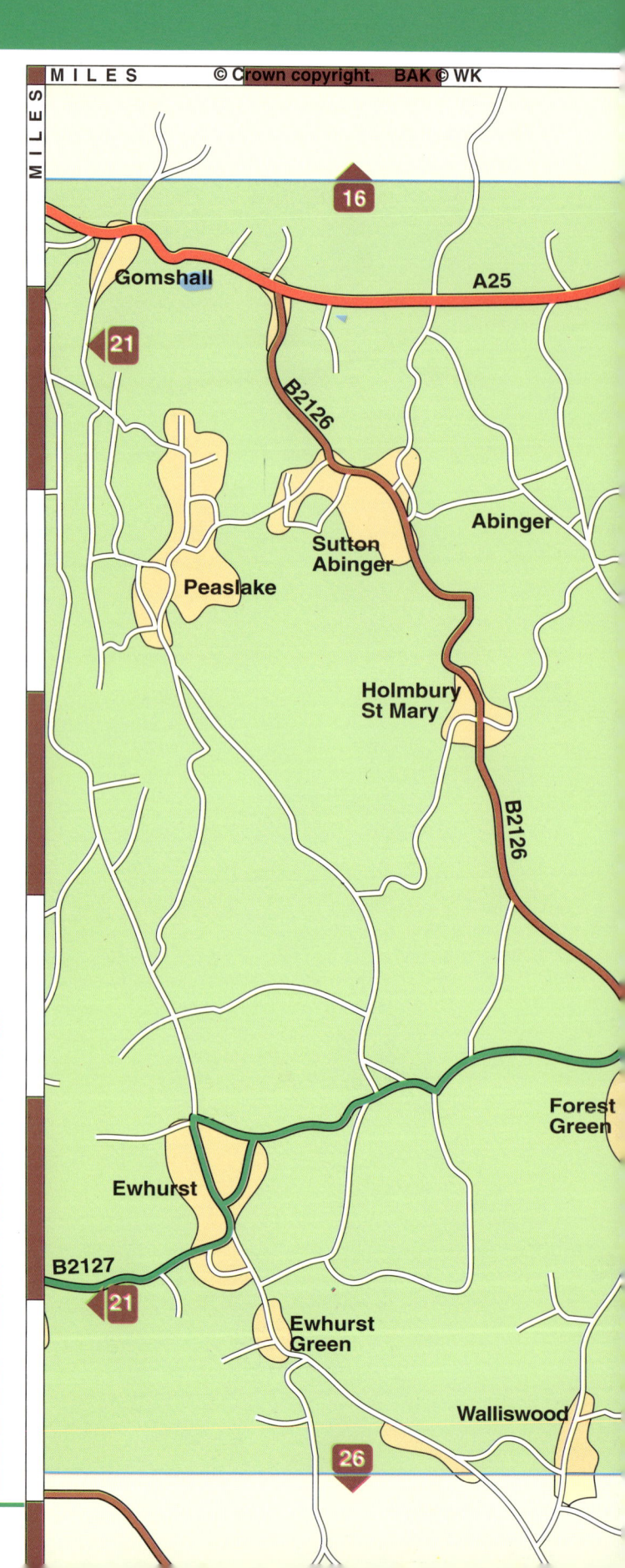

SOUTH OF DORKING 22

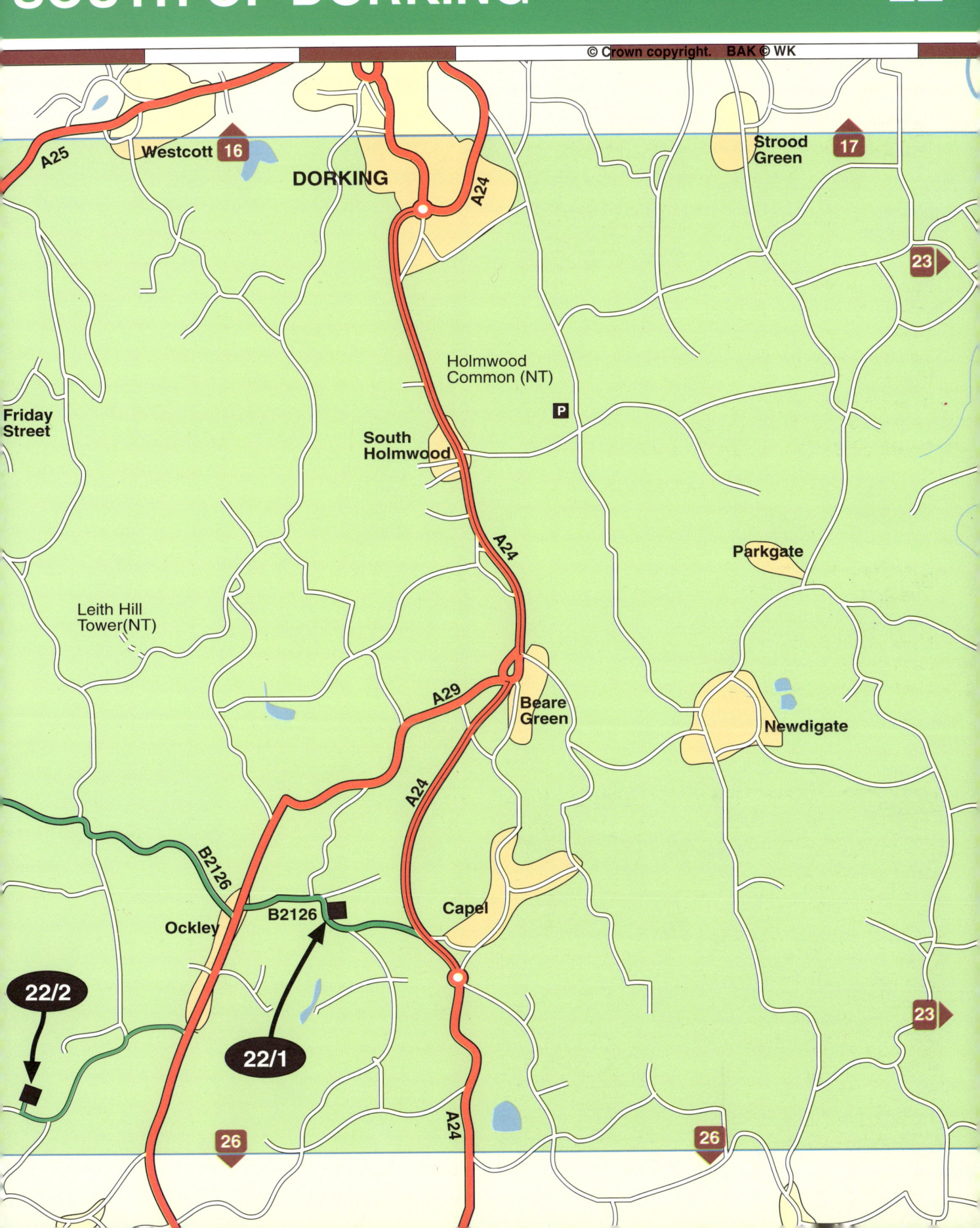

SURREY

NURSERIES & GARDEN CENTRES

23/1 NUTFIELD NURSERIES
Crabhill Lane, South Nutfield,
Redhill, Surrey RH1 5PC
01737 – 823 277

23/2 HILLSIDE SHRUBS AND HARDY PLANTS NURSERY
109 Horley Road, Earlswood,
Redhill, Surrey RH1 5AS
01737 – 765 645

23/3 SNOW HILL GARDEN CENTRE
Snow Hill,
Copthorne, Surrey RH10 3EV
01342 – 712 545

23/4 DOVES BARN NURSERY
Copthorne Road,
Felbridge, Surrey RH19 2PA

23/5 JACKSWOOD GARDEN CENTRE
Copthorne Road,
Crawley, West Sussex RH10 3PE
01293 – 883 311

WATER GARDEN CENTRE

23/6 NEWLAKE GARDENS
West Park Road,
Copthorne,
Crawley,
West Sussex
RH10 3HQ
01342 – 712 332

Water garden specialists. Growers of water lilies and water plants. Liners, pumps etc. Pool construction.
Open: October – March: Mondays – Saturdays, 9.30 – 4.30 (CLOSED SUNDAYS). April – September: Mondays – Saturdays 9.30 – 5.30, Sundays 11 – 5. Please phone for Christmas and Easter opening.
Wheelchairs: Good access.
Toilets: Ask if desperate.   **Dogs:** No.
Credit cards: Yes.

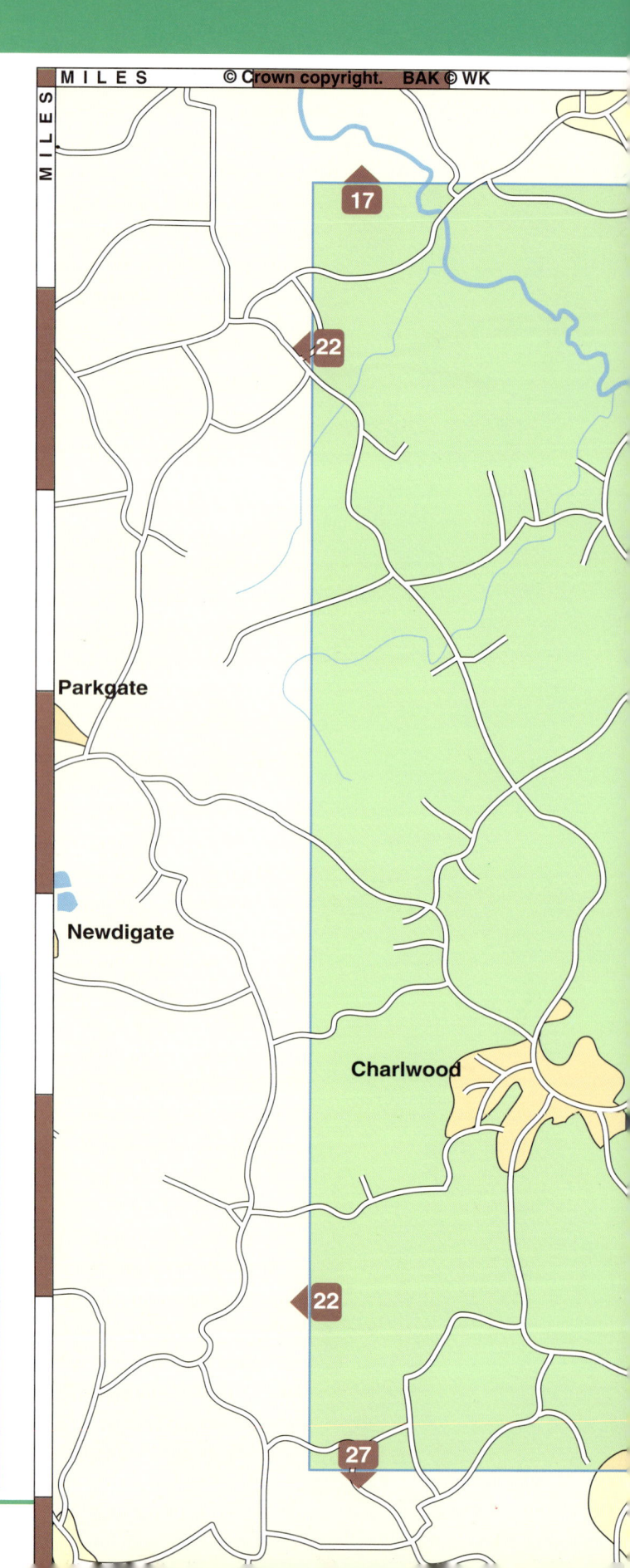

Road Atlas for Gardeners

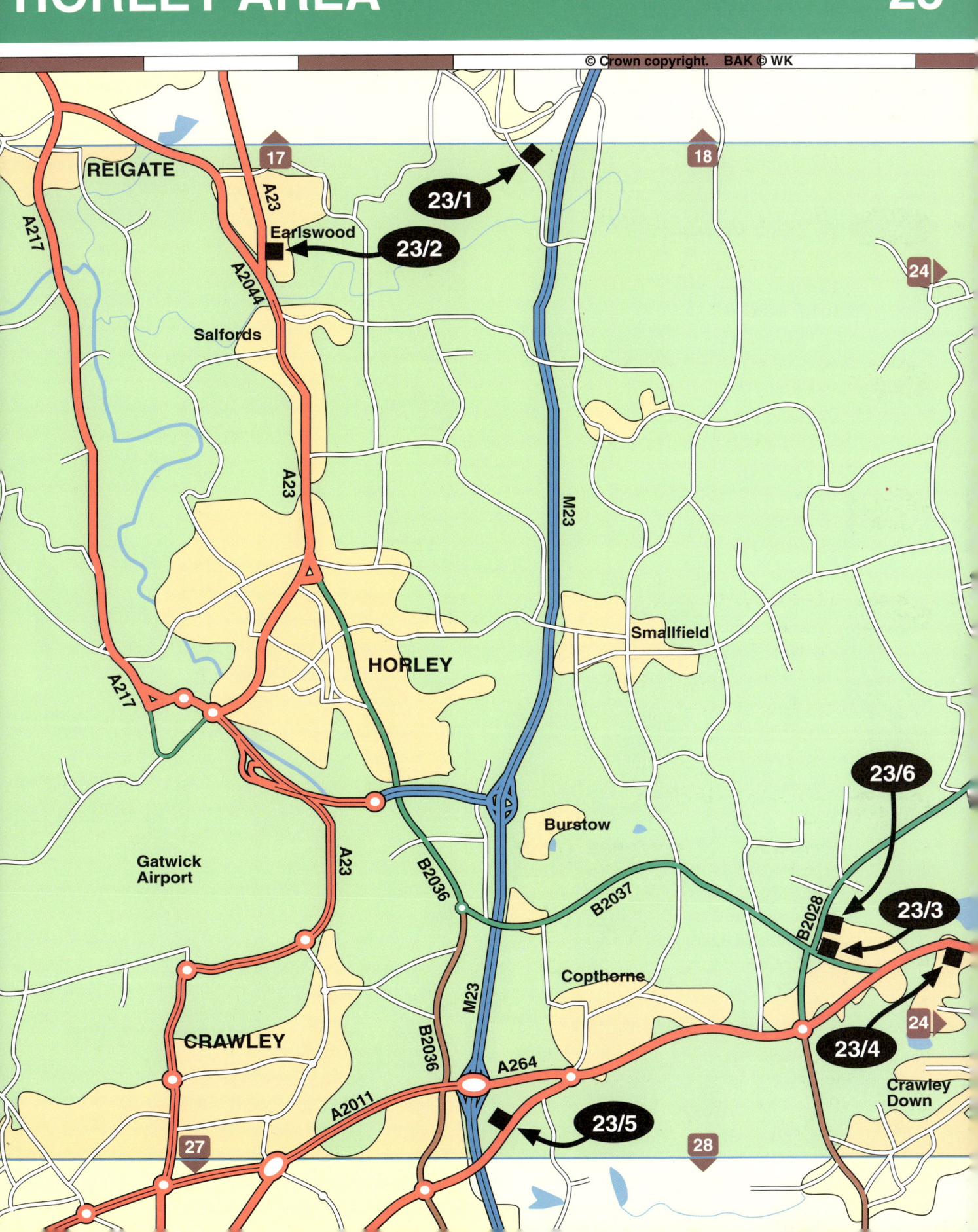

HORLEY AREA 23

SURREY

NURSERIES & GARDEN CENTRES

24/1 WOODHAM NURSERY
Eastbourne Road,
South Godstone, Surrey RH9 8EZ
01342 – 892 331

24/2 BROOK NURSERY AND PLANT CENTRE
Eastbourne Road,
South Godstone, Surrey RH9 8JF
01342 – 893 265

24/3 WALKERS GARDEN LEISURE
Anglefield Corner, Eastbourne Road (A22)
South Godstone, Surrey RH9 8JG
01342 – 893 109
A well established family-run centre for all garden, leisure and water gardening products.
Open: 7 days a week, Mondays – Saturdays 9 – 5.30, Sundays 10.30 – 4.30.
Toilets: Yes.   **Dogs:** On lead.   **Credit cards:** Yes.

24/4 OCCASIONALLY YOURS
Lingfield Common Road,
Lingfield,
Surrey RH7 6BZ
01342 – 833 937 
One of the largest selections of plants in the S.E. Farm shop, children's play area, animal corner, craft fairs.
Open: All year except Christmas and Boxing Days. 7 days a week, weekdays: winter 8.30 – 5.30; summer 8.30 – 6. Sundays all year 10.30 – 4.30.
Wheelchairs: Good access.
Toilets: Yes.   **Dogs:** On lead.   **Credit cards:** Yes.

24/5 WILLOW TREE NURSERY
Newchapel Road,
Lingfield, Surrey RH7 6BL
0342 – 834 961

24/6 HERONS BONSAI NURSERY
Wiremill Lane,
Newchapel,
Near Lingfield,
Surrey RH7 6HJ
01342 – 832 657 
'Britain's premier bonsai nursery.'
Open: All year except Christmas Day. 7 days a week: weekdays, winter 9 – dusk; summer 9 – 5.30. Sundays 10 – 4.30.
Wheelchairs: Yes.
Toilets: Yes.   **Dogs:** No.   **Credit cards:** Yes.

24/7 WYEVALE GARDEN CENTRE
Copthorne Road, Felbridge,
East Grinstead, West Sussex RH19 2PE
01342 – 328 881

24/8 LAURENCE HOBBS ORCHIDS
Bailiffs Cottage Nursery,
Hophurst Lane,
Crawley Down,
W. Sussex RH10 4LN
01342 – 715 142 
Orchids for growing in the home or heated greenhouse. Mail order service available – send SAE for catalogue.
Open: All year except Christmas, Boxing and New Years Days. 6 days a week (CLOSED FRIDAYS), 10 – 1, 2 – 5.
Wheelchairs: Yes.
Toilets: Ask if desperate.   **Dogs:** On lead.
Credit cards: Yes.

24/9 ORCHARD NURSERY
Holtye Road,
East Grinstead, West Sussex RH19 3PR
01342 – 311 657

WATER GARDEN CENTRE

24/10 BEAVER WATER PLANT AND FISH FARM
Beaver Farm, Eastbourne Road,
Newchapel,
Lingfield, Surrey RH7 6HL
01342 – 833 144

Road Atlas for Gardeners

GODSTONE – EAST GRINSTEAD　　24

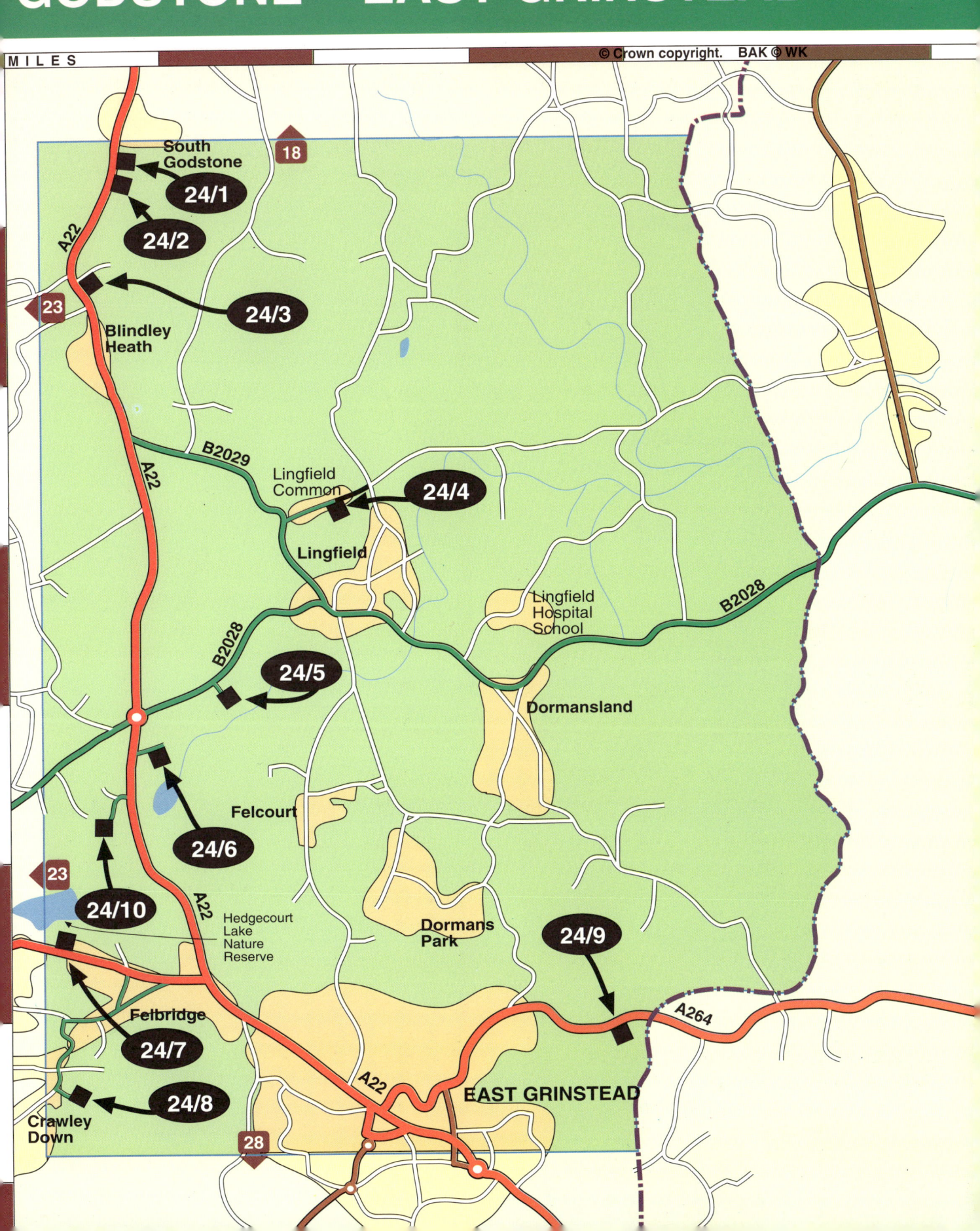

© Crown copyright.　BAK © WK

MILES

- South Godstone — 24/1
- 24/2
- 24/3
- Blindley Heath
- [23]
- [18]
- B2029
- Lingfield Common — 24/4
- Lingfield
- A22
- B2028
- 24/5
- Lingfield Hospital School
- Dormansland
- B2028
- Felcourt
- 24/6
- 24/10
- [23]
- A22
- Hedgecourt Lake Nature Reserve
- Dormans Park
- 24/9
- A264
- Felbridge
- 24/7
- 24/8
- Crawley Down
- EAST GRINSTEAD
- A22
- [28]

SURREY & WEST SUSSEX

NURSERIES & GARDEN CENTRES

25/1 ALFOLD GARDEN CENTRE
Cranleigh, Surrey
01403 – 752 359

25/2 LOXWOOD NURSERIES
Guildford Road,
Loxwood, West Sussex
01403 – 753389

GARDEN

25/3 RAMSTER

Open: 15 April – 30 July. 7 days a week 2 – 6.
Costs: Adults, £2.00; children, free.

Paul Temple

Road Atlas for Gardeners

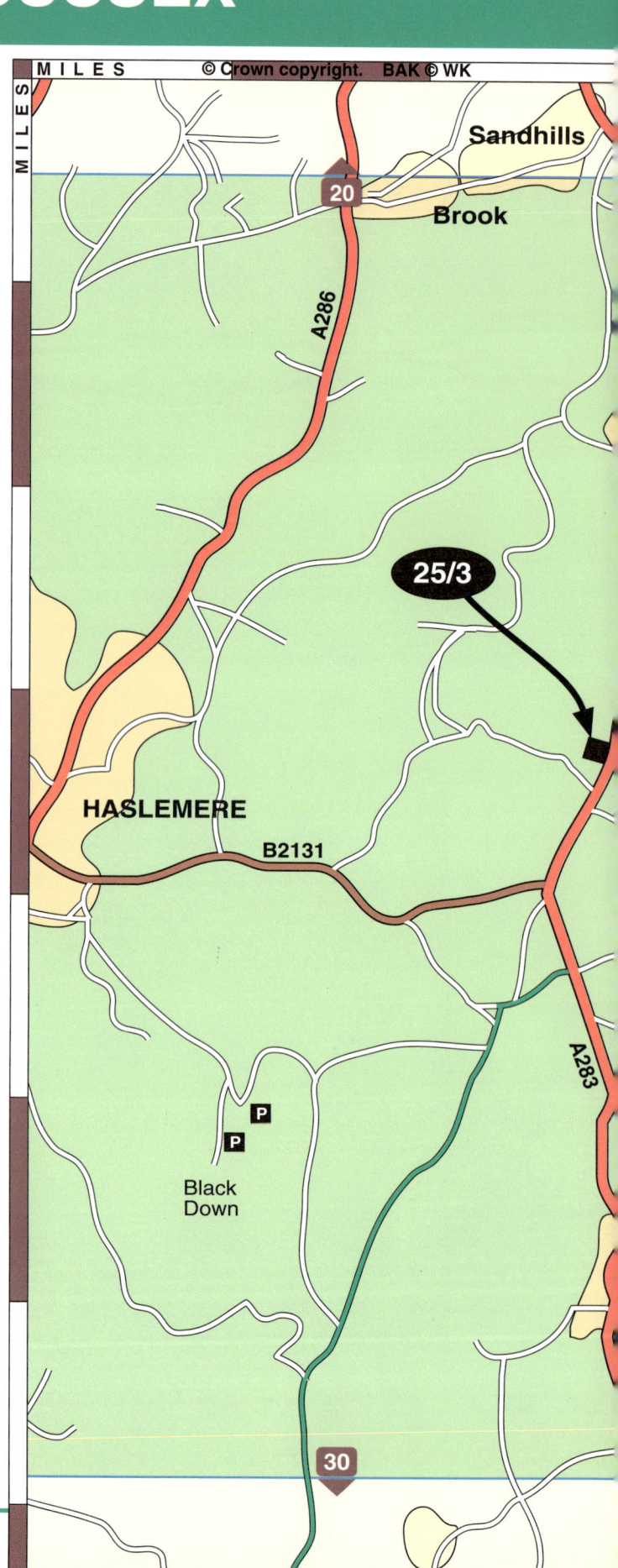

SOUTH WEST OF CRANLEIGH 25

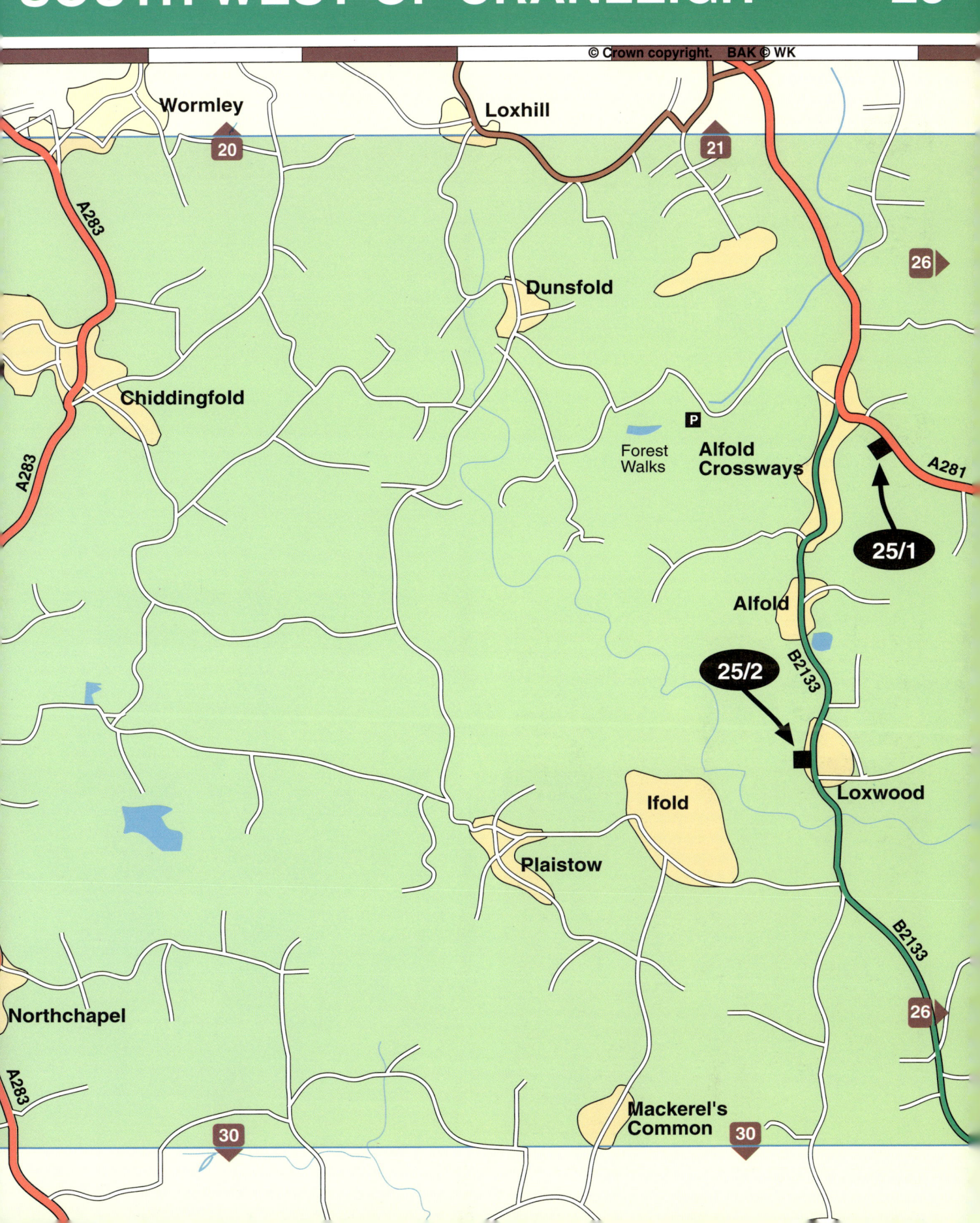

WEST SUSSEX

NURSERIES & GARDEN CENTRES

26/1 **NEWBRIDGE NURSERIES**
Billingshurst Road, Broadbridge Heath,
Horsham, West Sussex RH12 3LM
01403 – 265 731

26/2 **BOURNE HILL NURSERY**
Worthing Road,
Southwater, West Sussex RH13 7AS
01403 – 730 321

26/3 **HILLIER GARDEN CENTRE**
Brighton Road,
Horsham, West Sussex RH13 6QB
01403 – 210 113

Road Atlas for Gardeners

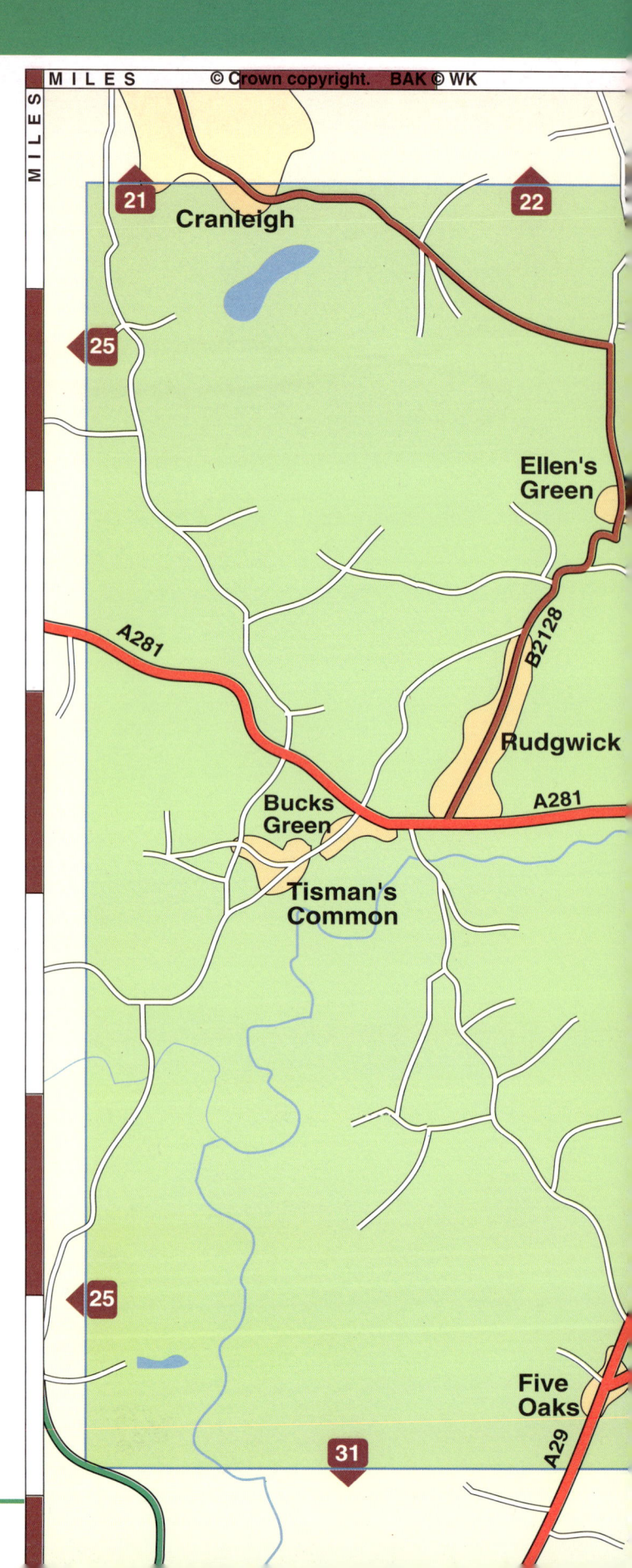

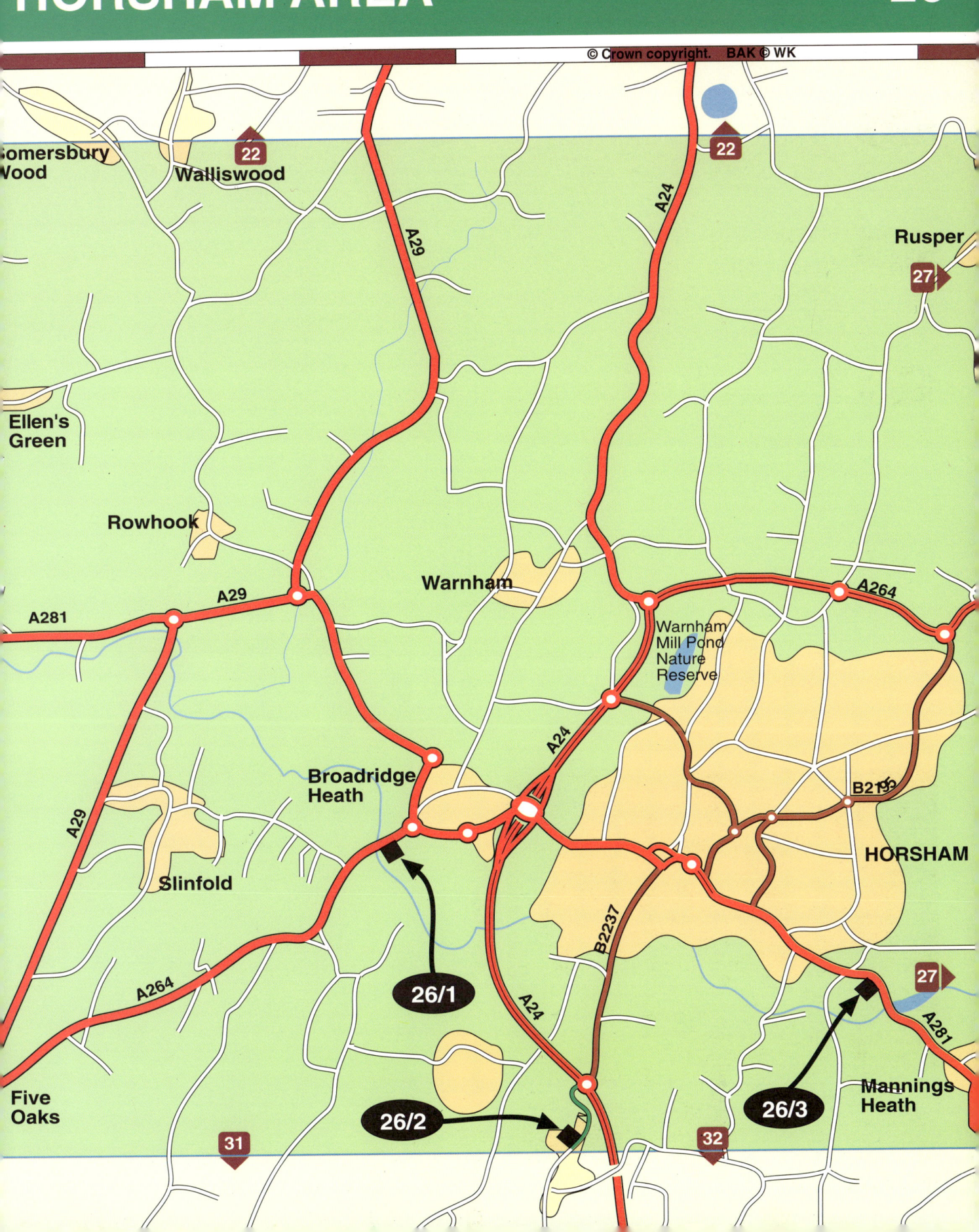

HORSHAM AREA 26

WEST SUSSEX

NURSERIES & GARDEN CENTRES

27/1 **HOMEBASE**

27/2 **B & Q**

27/3 **CHEALS GARDEN CENTRE**
Horsham Road,
Crawley,
West Sussex RH11 8PM
01293 – 522 101

27/4 **HOWARDS NURSERY CENTRE**
Plummers Plain,
Horsham,
West Sussex RH13 6NY
01403 – 891 565

27/5 **HIGH BEECHES NURSERIES**
Handcross,
Haywards Heath,
West Sussex RH17 6HO
01444 – 401 398

GARDENS

27/6 **HIGH BEECHES GARDENS**
01444 – 400 589
Open: Open spring and autumn: phone for dates.
Costs: Adults, £3.00; children, free.

27/7 **NYMANS GARDEN (NT)**
Handcross,
Haywards Heath,
West Sussex   RH17 6EB
01444 – 400 321 or 400 002

Rare and beautiful trees, shrubs and plants from all corners of the world. A delight from early spring to autumn. Tea room. Shop plant sales.
Open: March – end October, 5 days a week (CLOSED MONDAYS AND TUESDAYS but open Bank Holiday Mondays), 11 – 7 or sunset if earlier. Last admission 1 hour before closing.
Costs: Adults, £3.80.
Wheelchairs: Paths suitable for wheelchairs. Braille guide. Scented flowers and plants for visually impaired visitors. There are disabled toilets.
Toilets: Yes.   **Dogs:** In car park only.

Road Atlas for Gardeners

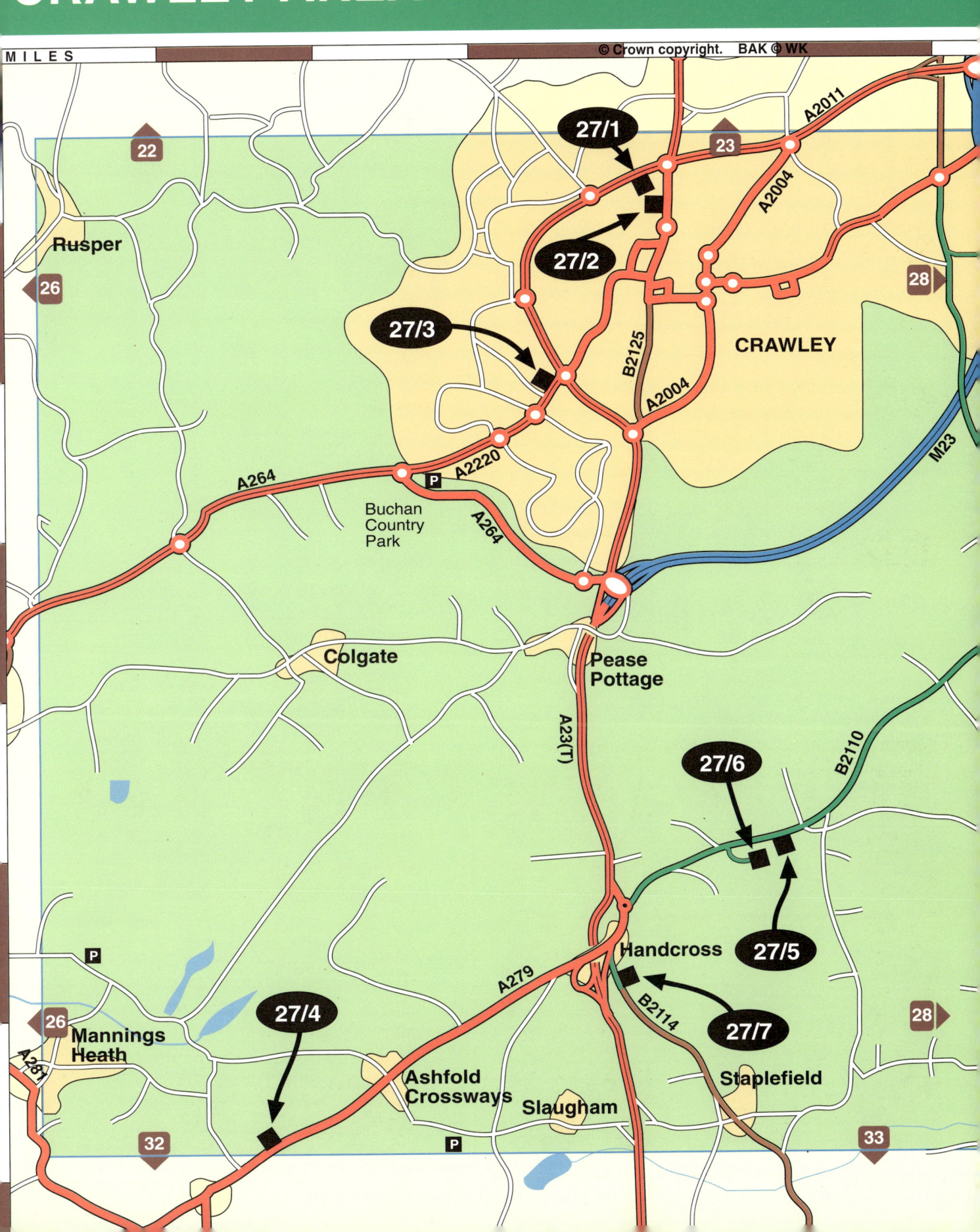

CRAWLEY AREA   27

WEST SUSSEX

WATER GARDEN CENTRE

28/1 WORLD OF WATER
Turners Hill Road,
Worth, Crawley,
West Sussex
RH10 4PE
01293 – 883 237

Large aquatic centre with 20+ display gardens. Specialists in water gardening and tropical fish. Free advice.
Open: All year except Christmas and Boxing Days. 7 days a week. Weekdays 1 November–31 January, 9–5; 1 February – 30 October, 9 – 6; Sunday all year 10.30 – 4.30.
Wheelchairs: Easy paved access with ramps.
Toilets: Yes.   **Dogs:** On lead.   **Credit cards:** Yes.

NURSERIES & GARDEN CENTRES

28/2 PLANTS 'N' GARDENS
World of Water,
Turners Hill Road,
Worth, Crawley
West Sussex
RH10 4PE
01293 – 882 992

Newly opened garden centre offering friendly, expert advice. Specialists in herbaceous plants and ornamental grasses.
Open: All year except Christmas, Boxing and New Year's Days. 7 days a week.
Winter: Mondays – Saturdays 9 – 5. Summer 9 – 6. Sundays all year 10.30 – 4.30.
Wheelchairs: Easy paved access with ramps.
Toilets: Yes.   **Dogs:** On lead.   **Credit cards:** Yes.

28/3 W.E.Th. INGWERSEN LTD
Birch Farm Nursery, Gravetye,
East Grinstead, West Sussex, RH19 4LE
01342 – 810 236

An award winning hardy plant nursery, specialising in alpines, rock plants, dwarf shrubs and conifers.
Open: 1 March – 30 September: 7 days a week, Mondays – Fridays 9 – 1 and 1.30 – 4, Saturdays, Sundays and Bank Holidays 10 – 1 and 1.30 – 4. Winter: Mondays – Fridays only.
Wheelchairs: Access possible, but on a hillside. Assistance available.
Toilets: Yes.   **Dogs:** On lead.   **Credit cards:** No.

PICK-YOUR-OWN FARM

28/4 TULLYS FARM
Turners Hill Road,
Turners Hill, West Sussex

GARDEN ARTEFACTS

28/5 POTS AND PITHOI
The Barns,
East Street,
Turners Hill,
West Sussex
RH10 4QQ
01342 – 714 793

Handmade terracotta pots from Crete for the garden, patio and conservatory. Up to 5ft high. Huge choice.
Open: All year except Christmas – New Year. 7 days a week, 10 – 5.
Wheelchairs: Yes.
Toilets: Yes.   **Dogs:** No.   **Credit cards:** Yes.

GARDENS

28/6 STANDEN (NT)
Open: 1 April – end October; Wednesdays – Sundays (CLOSED MONDAYS AND TUESDAYS), 12.30 – 6.
Costs: Adults (garden only): weekdays £2.50, weekends & Bank Holidays £3; children, weekdays £1.25, weekends & Bank Holidays £1.50. **Wheelchairs:** Part of garden accessible. Wheelchairs available.

28/7 WAKEHURST PLACE
Ardingly,
Near Haywards Heath,
West Susscx,
RH17 6TN
01444 – 892 701
(24 hour enquiry line 0181 – 332 5066)

National Botanic Garden noted for one of the finest collections of rare trees & flowering shrubs. Restaurant.
Open: All year except Christmas & New Year's Days; November – January 10 – 4, February 10 – 5, March & October 10 – 6, April – September 10 – 7.
Costs: Adults, £4.00; children, £1.50; senior citizens, £2.00; **Wheelchairs:** Good access. Wheelchairs are available on free loan.
Toilets: Yes.   **Dogs:** No.   **Credit cards:** No.

Road Atlas for Gardeners

CRAWLEY – EAST GRINSTEAD 28

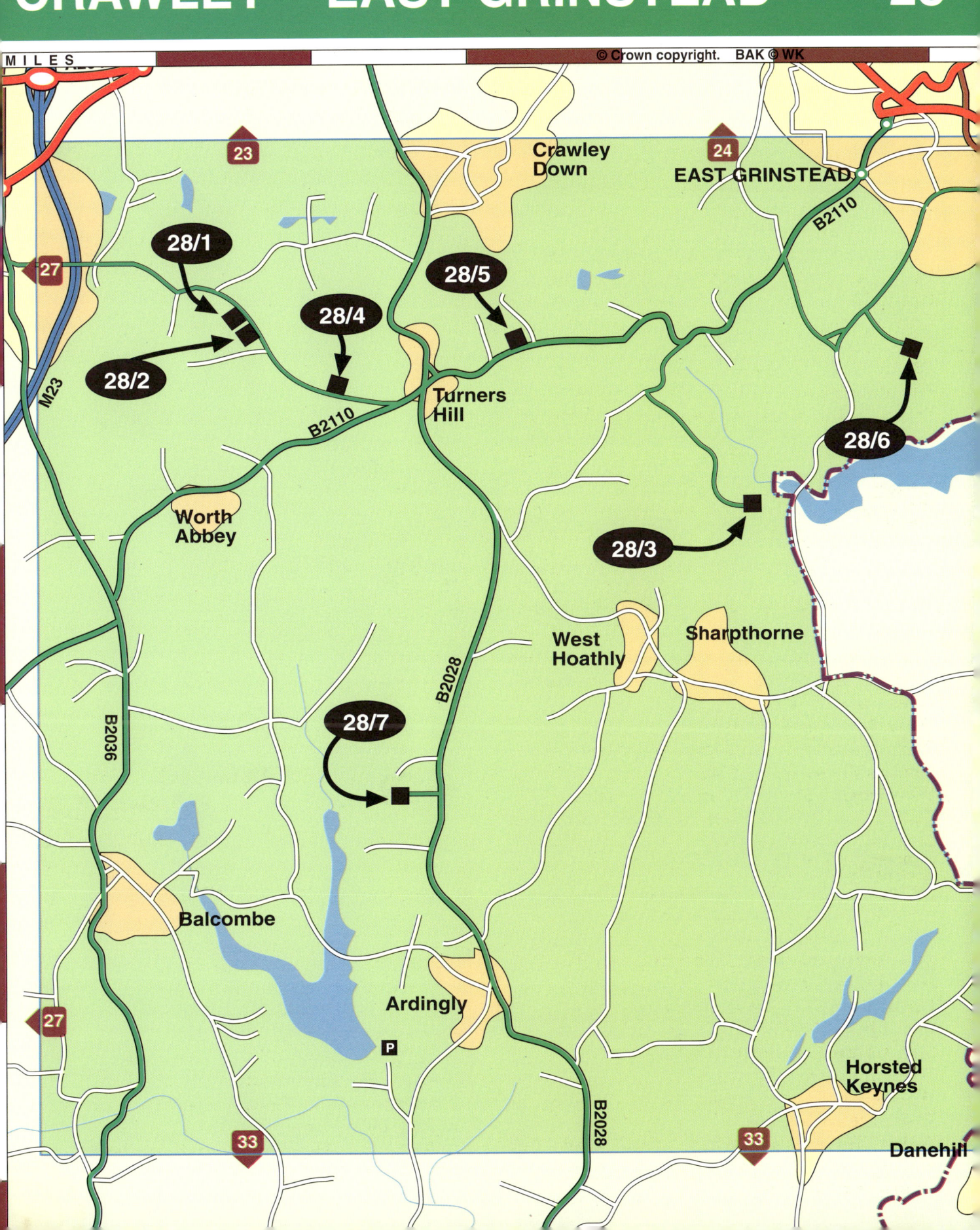

WEST SUSSEX

NURSERIES & GARDEN CENTRES

29/1 ROTHERHILL NURSERIES AND GARDEN CENTRE
Stedham,
Midhurst, West Sussex GU29 0PB
01370 – 813 687

29/2 AYLINGS OF TROTTON
Trotton, Rogate,
Petersfield, Hampshire GU31 5ES
01730 – 813 621
Very large range of shrubs and herbaceous plants, terracotta, ceramics and pot plants. Teas at weekends.
Open: All year except Christmas and Boxing Days (open other Bank Holidays).
Mondays – Saturdays 8 – 5, Sundays 10.30 – 4.30.
Wheelchairs: There is access for wheelchairs.
Toilets: Yes. **Dogs:** On lead. **Credit cards:** Yes.

GARDENS

29/3 FITZHALL
Iping, near Midhurst,
West Sussex GU29 0JR
01730 – 813 634
Open: All year except Christmas and Boxing Days. 7 days a week.
Costs: Adults, £1.50; children, 75p.

29/4 UPPARK (NT)

Open: 1 June – end October; Sundays – Thursdays (CLOSED FRIDAYS & SATURDAYS), 12 – 5.30. Note that entry to the car park and property will be restricted when crowded.
Costs: Adults, £5.00 including house; families, £12.50 including house.
Wheelchairs: Garden is accessible. Wheelchairs are available. There are disabled toilets.

Road Atlas for Gardeners

MIDHURST AREA 29

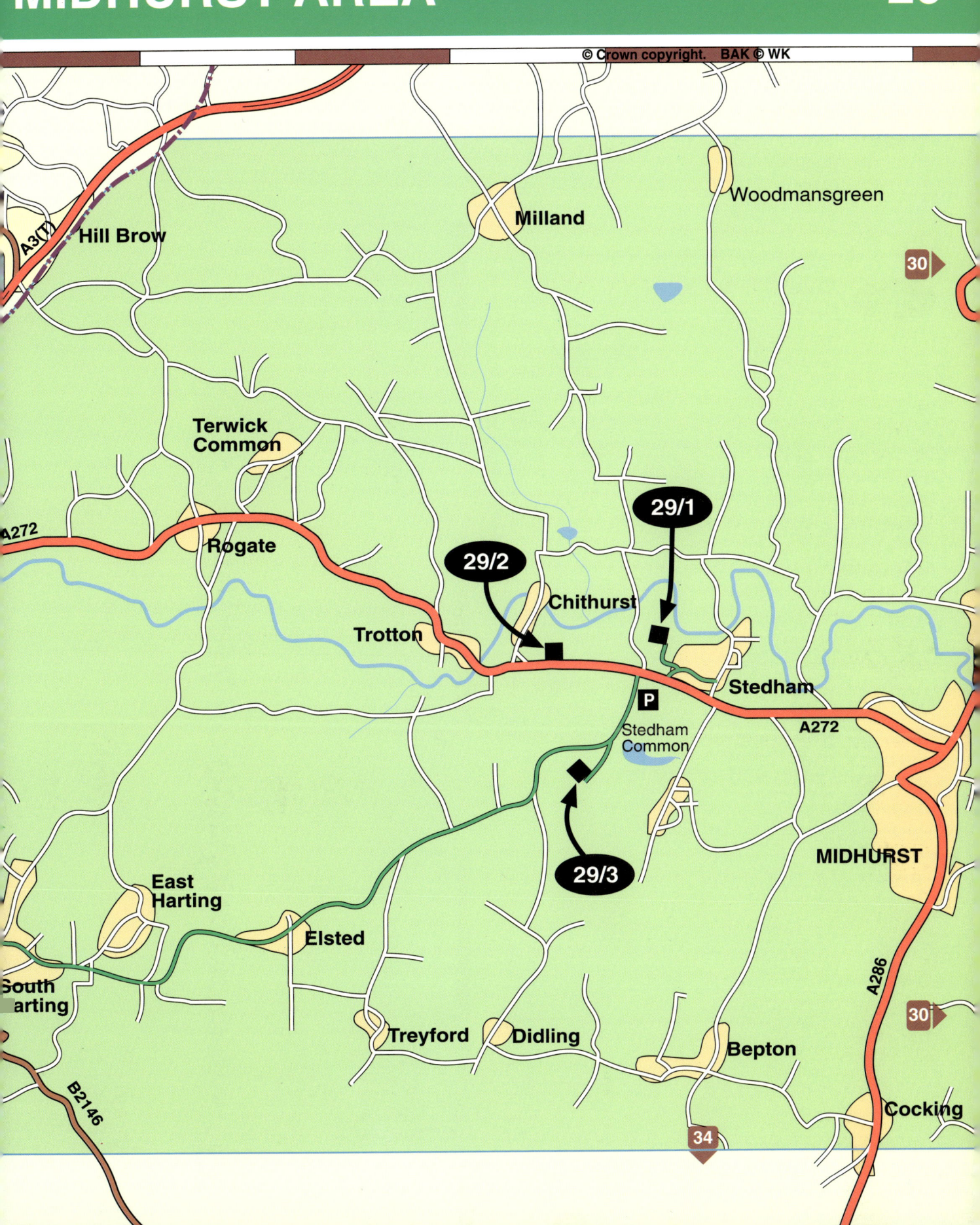

WEST SUSSEX

NURSERIES & GARDEN CENTRES

30/1 GRINSTEAD NURSERIES
London Road,
Petworth, West Sussex,
01798 – 343 877

30/2 RIVERVIEW GARDEN CENTRE
Stopham Road,
Pulborough,
West Sussex
RH20 1DS
01798 – 872 981

Comprehensive garden centre set in landscaped grounds; miniature railway, café, pet shop, swimming pools.
Open: All year except Christmas, Boxing and New Year's Days. 7 days a week. Mondays – Fridays 8.30 – 5.30, Saturdays 9 – 6 (January and February weekdays 9 – 5); Sundays 10.30 – 4.30.
Wheelchairs: Available, and all pathways suitable.
Toilets: Yes.   **Dogs:** On lead.   **Credit cards:** Yes.

GARDEN

30/3 PETWORTH PARK (NT)

Open: 7 days a week (except after 12 on 23 – 25 June), 8 – sunset.
Costs: Free. **Wheelchairs:** Part accessible with care.

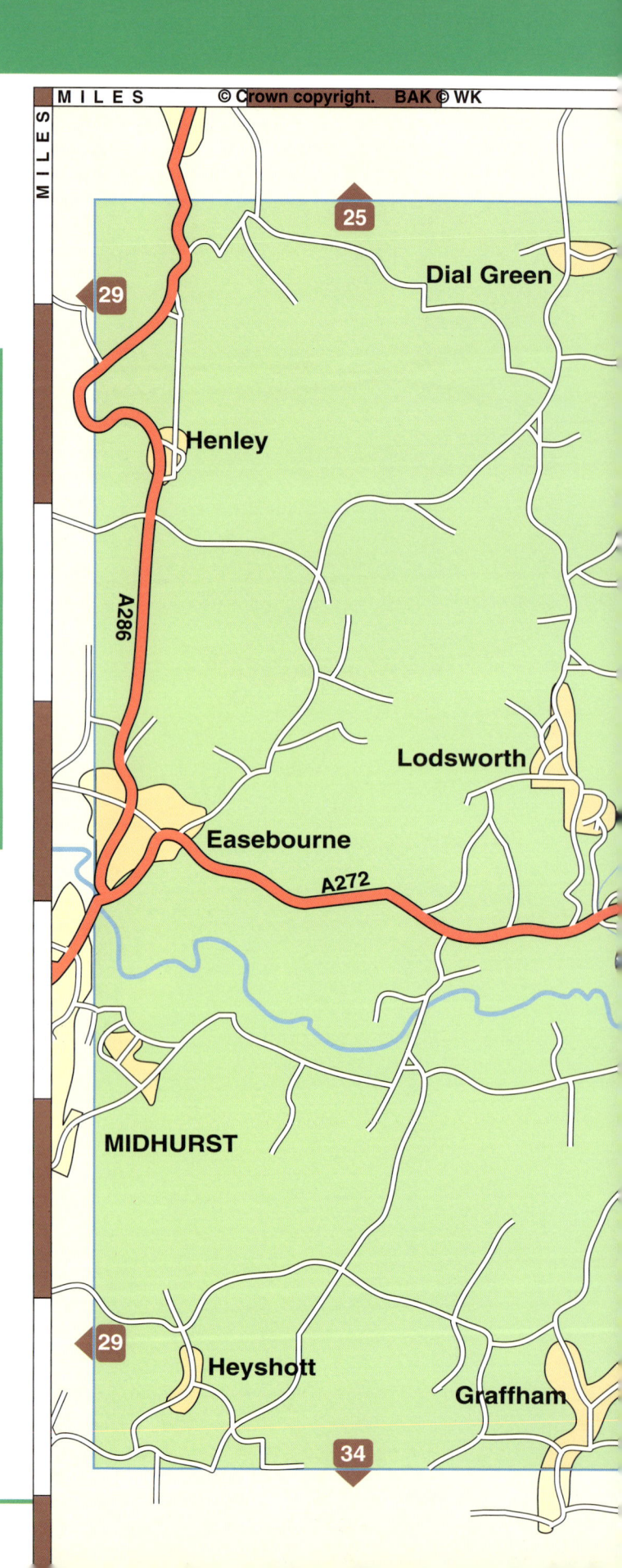

Road Atlas for Gardeners

PETWORTH AREA 30

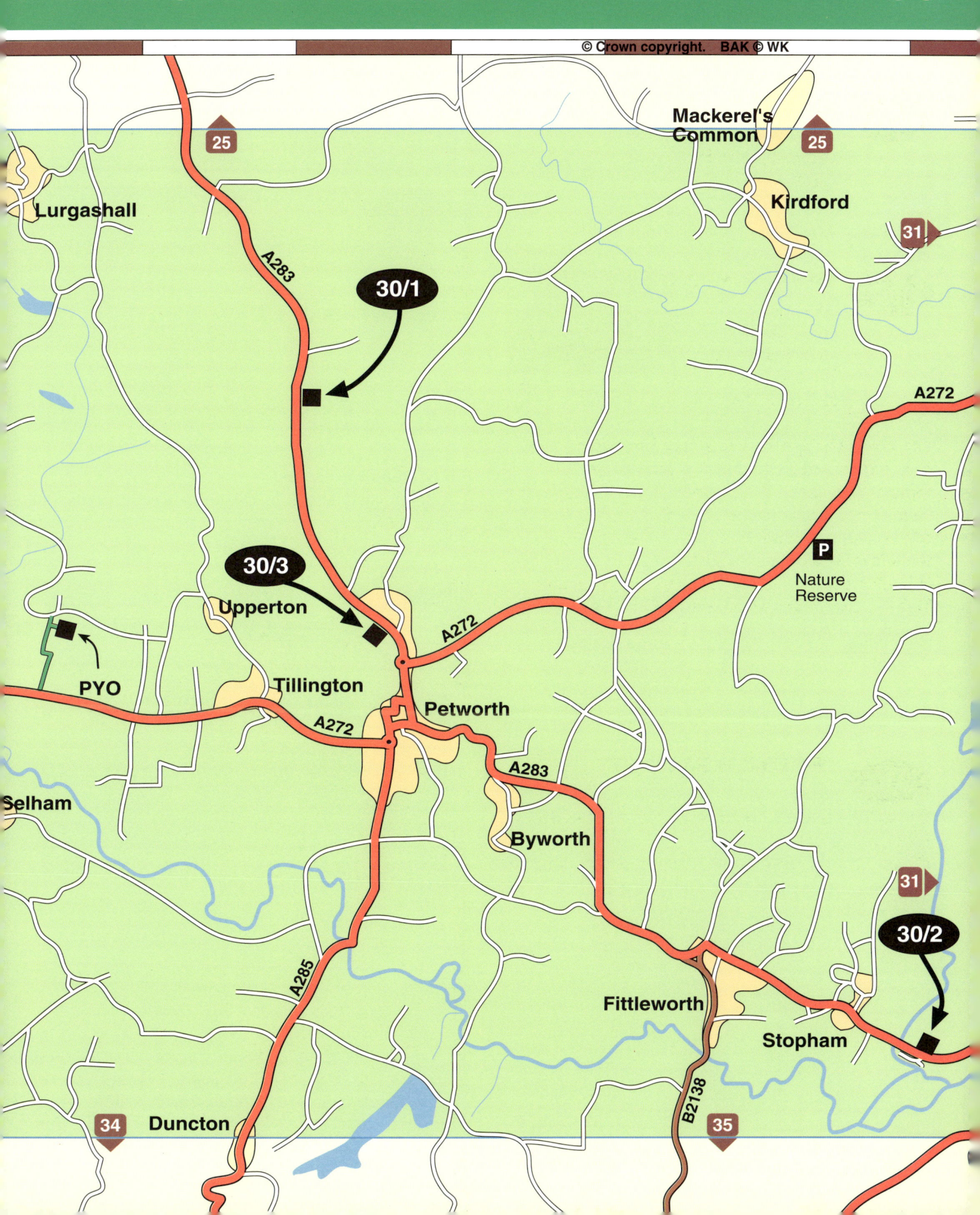

WEST SUSSEX

NURSERIES & GARDEN CENTRES

31/1 BLACKGATE LANE NURSERY
Blackgate Lane,
Pulborough, West Sussex
01798 – 872 923 or 813 521

31/2 MURRELLS NURSERY
Broomers Hill Lane,
Pulborough,
West Sussex
RH20 2DU
01798 – 875 508

Extensive range (incl. some unusual varieties) of shrubs, herbaceous, bedding, trees & fruit trees. Bonsai.
Open: All year except Christmas, Boxing and New Year's Days and Easter Sunday. 7 days a week.
Winter: Mondays – Saturdays 9 – 5, Sundays 10 – 4.
Summer: 9 – 5.30, Sundays 10 – 4.
Wheelchairs: Reasonable, with assistance.
Toilets: No.   **Dogs:** On lead.   **Credit cards:** Yes.

31/3 TANGLEWOOD
Kirdford Road, Wisborough Green,
Billingshurst, West Sussex RH14 0DD
01403 – 700 332

31/4 GREENWAYS NURSERY
Kirdford Road, Wisborough Green,
Billingshurst, West Sussex RH14 0DD

31/5 WALLABIES NURSERY
Kirdford Road, Wisborough,
Billingshurst, West Sussex RH14 0DD
01403 – 700 147

Specialities: wild flower plants; hanging baskets; summer and winter bedding plants.
Open: All year except Christmas and Boxing Days. 7 days a week, 9 – 5.
Wheelchairs: Paved access.
Toilets: Ask if desperate.   **Dogs:** On lead.
Credit cards: No.

31/6 ACE NURSERY
Coneyhurst Road,
Billingshurst, West Sussex

GARDEN & GARDEN CENTRE

31/7 COOMBLAND GARDENS
Coneyhurst,
Billingshurst, West Sussex RH14 9DY
01403 – 741 549

Interesting 5-acre garden. Roses, choice herbaceous plants. National collection of hardy geraniums.
Open: Nursery: March – end October weekdays 2 – 4 excluding Bank Holidays. Other times by appointment, please. Garden: June. Groups may be able to book a visit in the spring. Garden normally closed on Sundays.
Costs: Nursery free, garden £2.00.
Wheelchairs: Limited access.
Toilets: Ask if desperate. **Dogs:** No. **Credit cards:** No.

WATER GARDEN CENTRES

31/8 ARCHER-WILLS LTD
Broadford Bridge Road, West Chittington,
Pulborough, West Sussex RH20 2LE
01798 – 813 204

31/9 DANFIELD NURSERY AND ORNAMENTAL FISH FARM
Thakeham,
Nr Storrington, West Sussex RH20 2LO
01403 – 741 279

NURSERY & GARDEN

31/10 HOLLY GATE CACTUS NURSERY AND GARDEN
Billingshurst Road (B2133),
Ashington, West Sussex, RH20 3BA
01903 – 892 930

Leading grower of desert and tropical cactus & succulents, plus famous garden with over 50,000 exotic plants.
Open: All year except Christmas and Boxing Days. 7 days a week, 9 – 5.   **Costs:** Nursery, free. Garden: adults, £1.50; children, £1.00; senior citizens, £1.00.
Wheelchairs: Access to nursery and garden.
Toilets: Yes.   **Dogs:** On lead.   **Credit cards:** Yes.

Road Atlas for Gardeners

BILLINGSHURST – PULBOROUGH 31

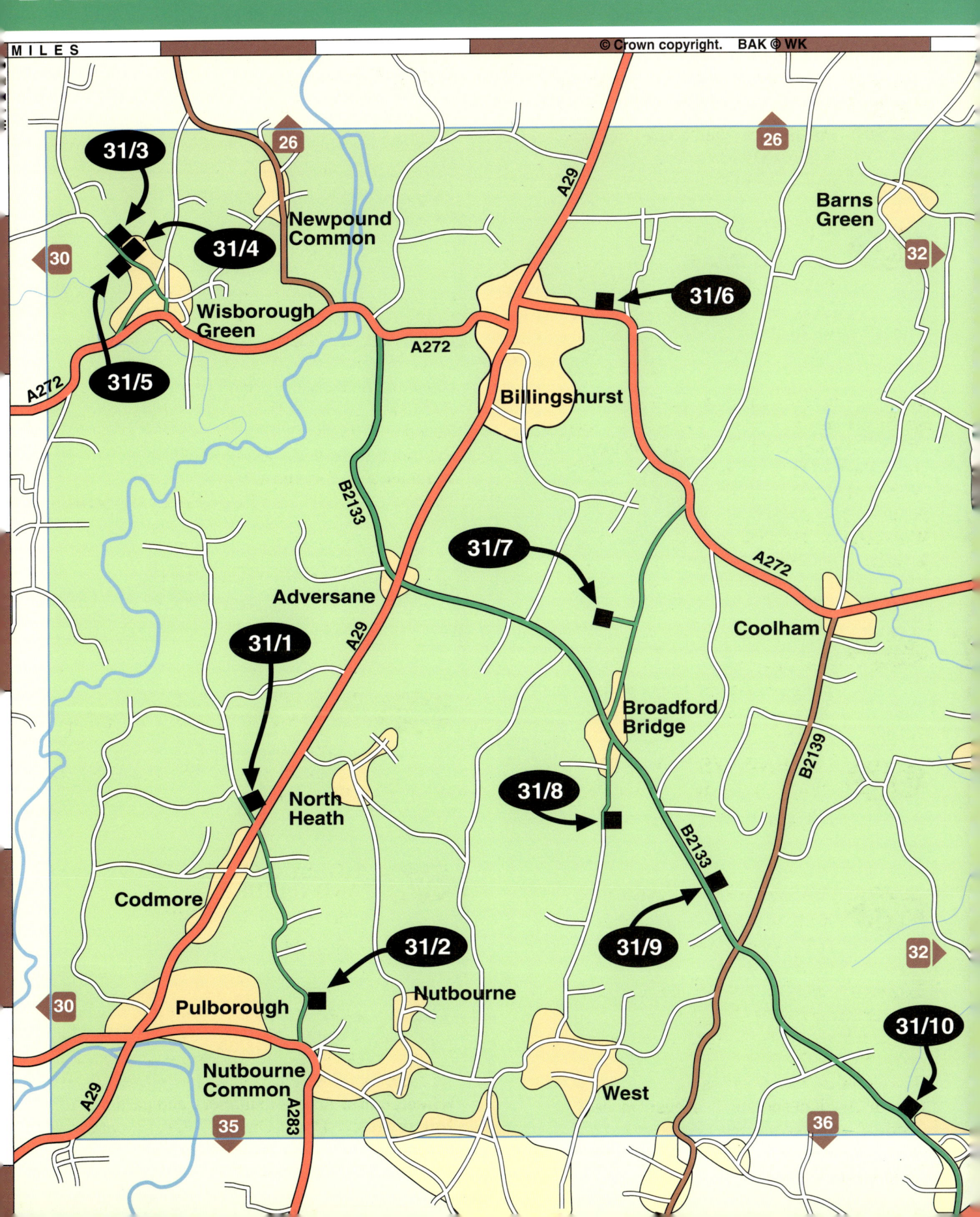

WEST SUSSEX

NURSERIES & GARDEN CENTRES

32/1 ARCHITECTURAL PLANTS
Cooks Farm, Nuthurst,
Horsham, West Sussex RH13 6LH
01403 – 891 772

32/2 CBF NURSERIES
Littleworth Lane, West Grinstead,
Horsham, West Sussex RH13 8NB
0403 – 864 773
Wheelchairs: There are disabled toilets.

32/3 OLD BARN NURSERIES
Worthing Road,
Dial Post,
Near Horsham,
West Sussex
RH13 8NR
01403 – 710 000

Modern retail nursery specialising in outdoor and indoor plants. Home-cooked food in the Old Barn Pantry.
Open: All year except Christmas and Boxing Days. Mondays – Saturdays 9 – 6, Sundays 10.30 – 4.30. Old Barn Pantry open daily, 9 – 6.
Wheelchairs: Easy access all on flat ground. Wheelchairs are available and there are disabled toilets.
Toilets: Yes.   **Dogs:** On lead.   **Credit cards:** Yes.

SEE PAGE 43 FOR FULL DETAILS

GARDEN

32/4 LEONARDSLEE GARDENS

Open: 1 April – 31 October. 7 days a week 10 – 6 (in May 10 – 8).
Costs: Adults, (May) £4.00, (rest of year) £3.00; children, £2.00.

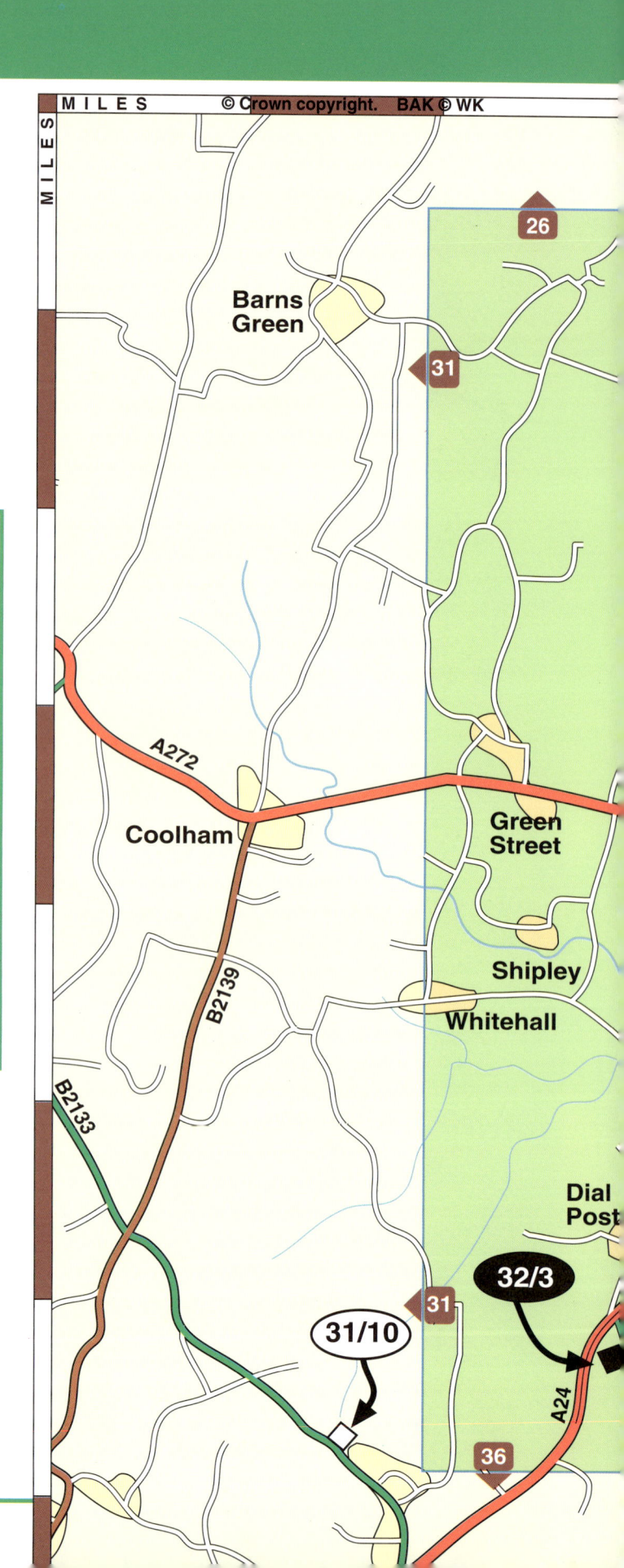

Road Atlas for Gardeners

SOUTH OF HORSHAM 32

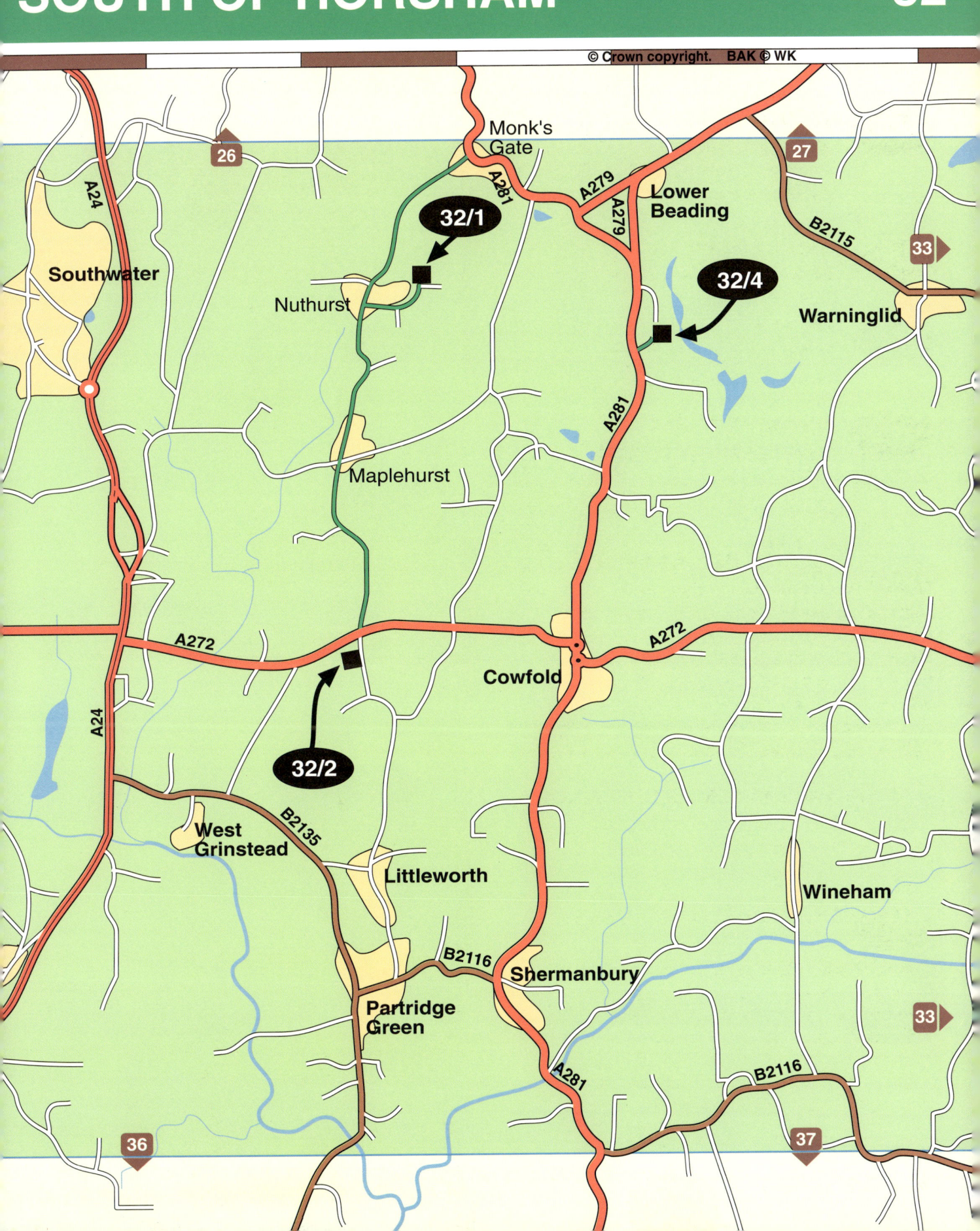

WEST SUSSEX

NURSERIES & GARDEN CENTRES

33/1 COUNTRY GARDENS AT HANDCROSS

33/2 STANBRIDGE VIEW NURSERY
London Road,
Handcross, West Sussex RH17 6BB
01444 – 461 266

33/3 BOLNEY NURSERY
Cowfold Road,
Bolney, West Sussex RH17 5QP
01444 – 881 784

33/4 MARYLANDS NURSERY
Bolney, West Sussex
01444 – 881 682

33/5 SCAYNES HILL NURSERY
Lewes Road,
Near Haywards Heath,
West Sussex RH7 7PC
01444 – 831 673

PICK-YOUR-OWN FARM

33/6 PATERNOSTERS FRUIT FARM
Sloughgreen Lane, Warninglid,
Near Cuckfield, West Sussex
01444 – 461 474

GARDEN

33/7 BORDE HILL GARDENS

Open: 18 March – 1 October, daily 10 – 6.
Costs: Adults, £3.50 (parkland only, £1.00); children, £1.50; senior citizens, £3.00.

Road Atlas for Gardeners

HAYWARDS HEATH AREA 33

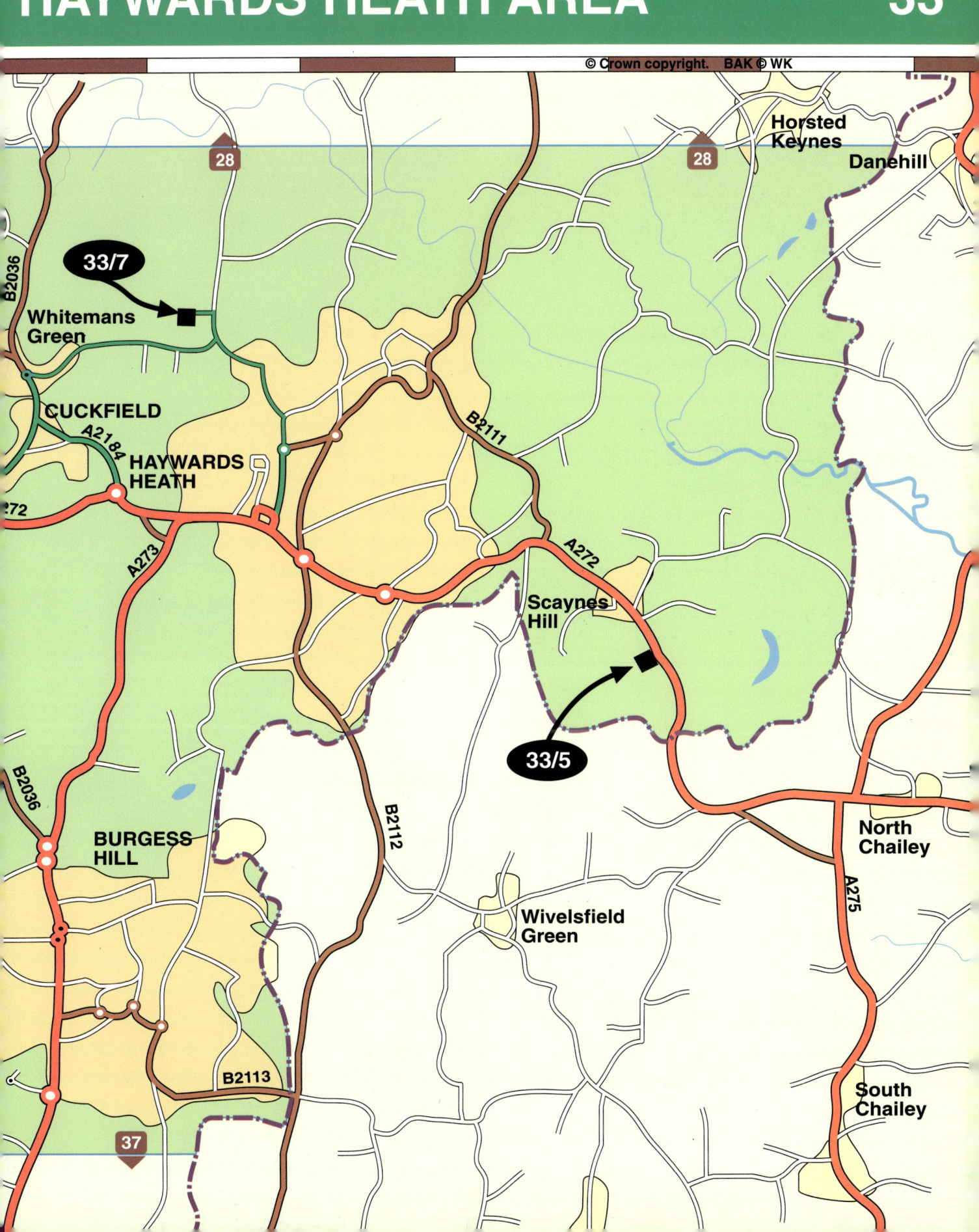

WEST SUSSEX

NURSERIES & GARDEN CENTRES

34/1 EAST ASHLING NURSERIES
Lye Lane, East Ashling,
Near Chichester, West Sussex P018 9DD
01243 – 575 523

34/2 PUMPKIN COTTAGE
The Lodge, 4 Top Road, Slindon,
Near Arundel, West Sussex BN18 0RR
01243 – 814 219

VINEYARD

34/3 CHILSDOWN VINEYARD
The Old Station, Singleton,
Chichester, West Sussex P018 0RY
01243 – 811 398

GARDEN

34/4 WEST DEAN GARDENS
West Dean,
Chichester,
West Sussex PO18 0QZ
01243 – 811 303

35-acre South Downs garden, 45-acre arboretum, 2.5-acre walled kitchen garden, historic glasshouses.
Open: 7 days a week, 1 April – 29 October, 11 – 5 (last tickets at 4).
Costs: Adults, £3.00; children, £1.50; senior citizens, £2.50; families, £8.00.
Wheelchairs: Yes. There are disabled toilets.
Toilets: Yes.   **Dogs:** No.   **Credit cards:** No.

SEE PAGE 43 FOR FULL DETAILS

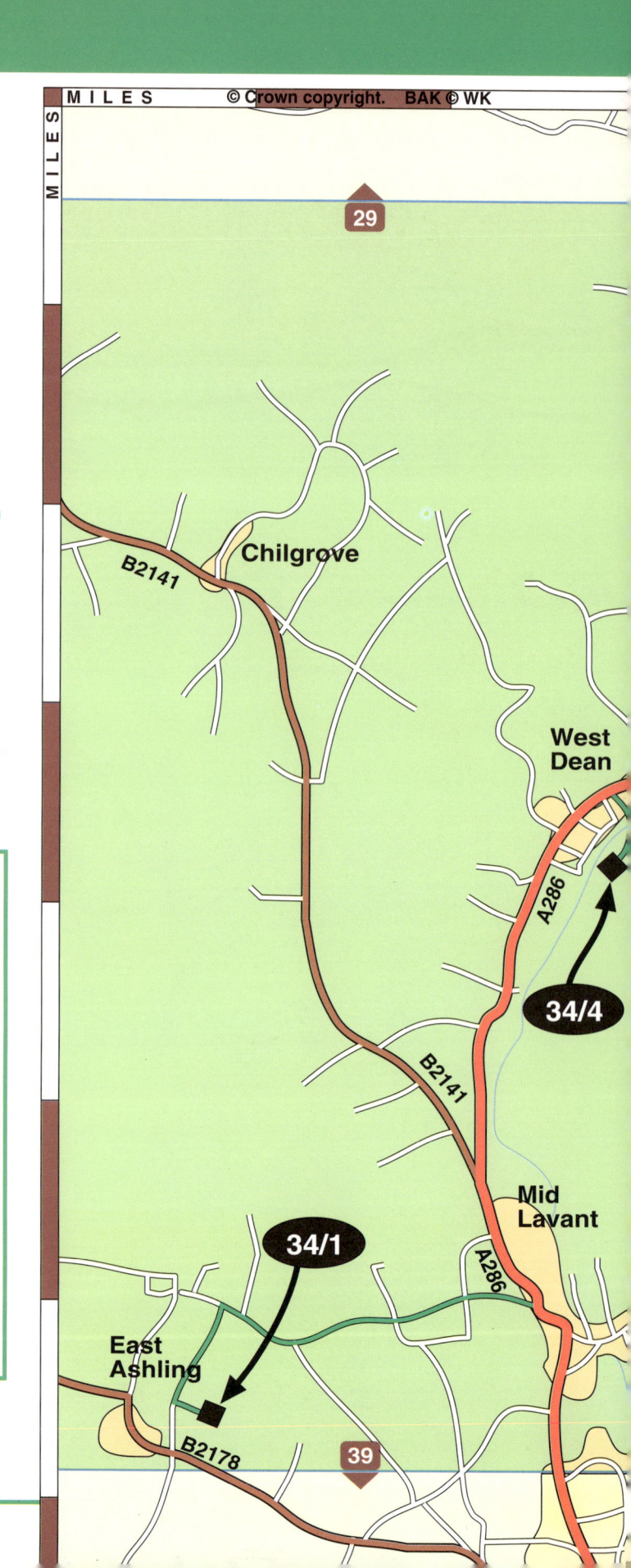

Road Atlas for Gardeners

GOODWOOD AREA 34

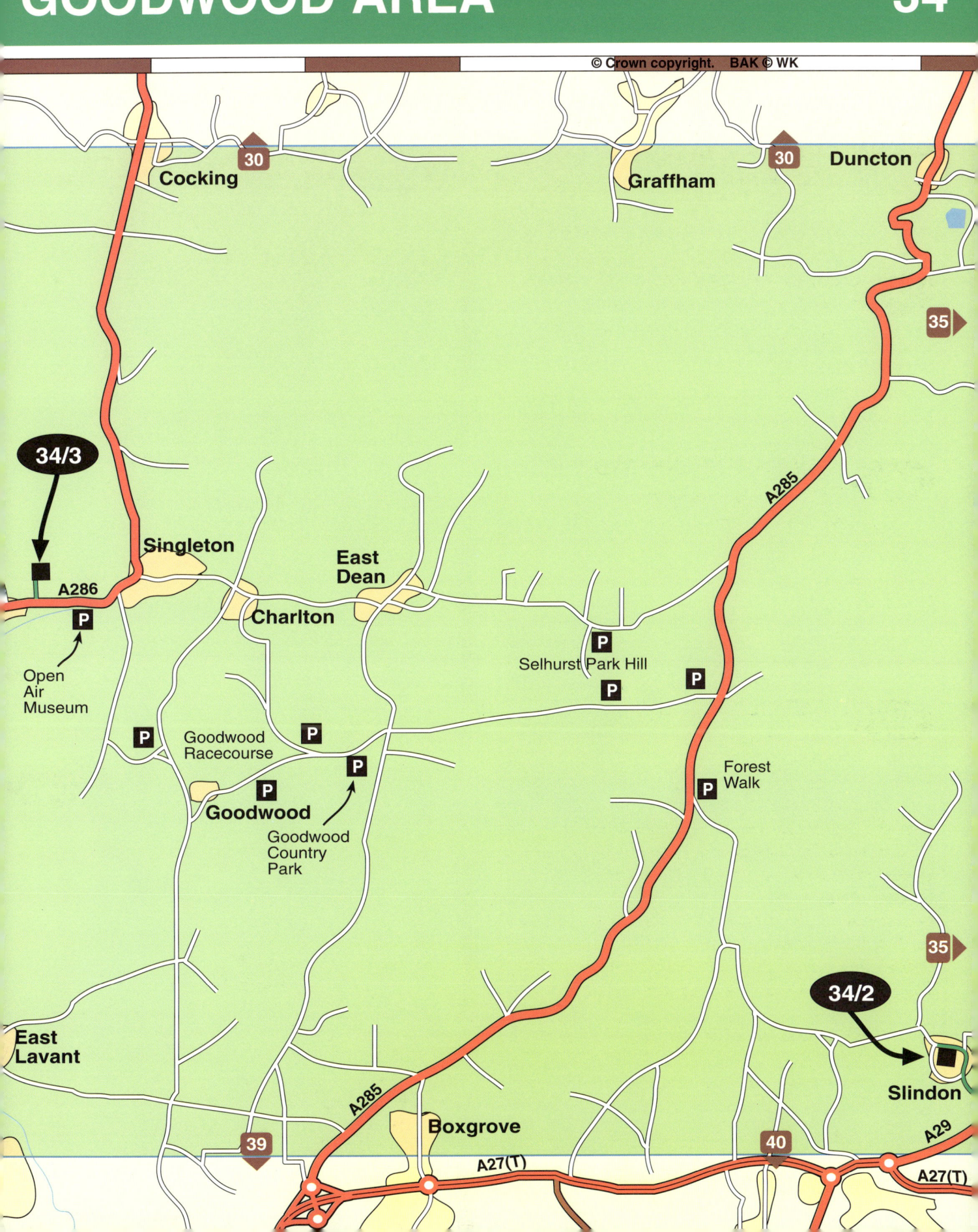

- Cocking 30
- Graffham
- Duncton 30
- 35
- 34/3
- Singleton
- A286
- Open Air Museum
- East Dean
- Charlton
- A285
- Selhurst Park Hill
- Goodwood Racecourse
- Goodwood
- Goodwood Country Park
- Forest Walk
- East Lavant
- A285
- Boxgrove
- 39
- 40
- 35
- 34/2
- Slindon
- A29
- A27(T)

© Crown copyright. BAK © WK

WEST SUSSEX

GARDEN

35/1 PARHAM ELIZABETHAN HOUSE AND GARDENS

Parham Park,
Pulborough, West Sussex RH20 4HS
01903 – 744 888

4-acre walled garden and seven acres of 18th century pleasure grounds. Home-grown plants for sale.

Open: Easter – October. Wednesdays, Thursdays, Sundays and Bank Holiday Mondays. AFTERNOONS ONLY.
Costs: Adults, garden only, £3.00; children, £1.50.
Wheelchairs: Paths in the 4-acre walled garden are suitable for wheelchairs.
Toilets: Yes.   **Dogs:** On lead.   **Credit cards:** No.

Gold border at Parham

Road Atlas for Gardeners

SOUTH OF PULBOROUGH 35

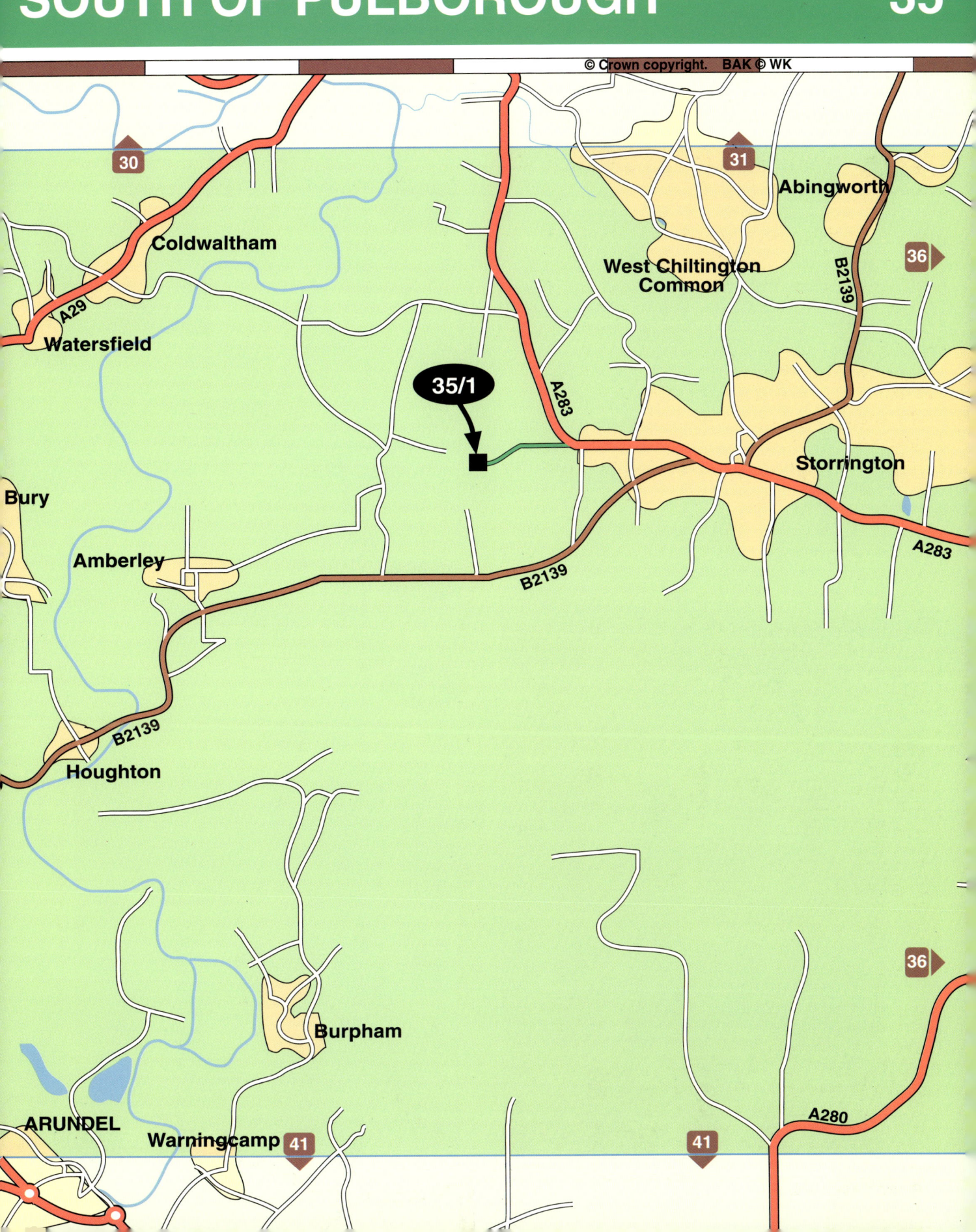

WEST SUSSEX

NURSERIES & GARDEN CENTRES

36/1 WASHINGTON GARDEN CENTRE (ENGLISH WATER GARDENS)
London Road,
Washington, West Sussex RH20 3BL
01903 – 892 006

A large garden centre specialising in trees, shrubs and water gardens. Stoneware. Pets. Coffee shop.
Open: All year except Christmas Day. 7 days a week, Mondays – Saturdays 9 – 5.30, Sundays 10.30 – 4.30.
Wheelchairs: Easy paved access, wheelchair available.
Toilets: Yes.   **Dogs:** On lead.   **Credit cards:** Yes.

36/2 HOLE STREET NURSERIES
Hole Street,
Ashington, West Sussex RH20 3DF
01903 – 892 897

36/3 THE OLD NURSERY GARDEN
Rock Road, Washington,
Near Pulborough, West Sussex RH20 3BI
01903 – 892 626

36/4 JACKSWOOD GARDEN CENTRE
Findon By-pass, Findon Village,
Near Worthing, West Sussex BN14 0RE
01903 – 874 111

36/5 BARROW HILL NURSERY
Shoreham Road,
Henfield,
West Sussex,
BN5 9DN
01273 – 492 733

A family-run nursery in a farmyard setting with a large selection of plants, mainly home produced.
Open: All year except Christmas – New Year. 7 days a week, 9 – 5.30.
Wheelchairs: Accessible.
Toilets: No.   **Dogs:** On lead.   **Credit cards:** Yes.

PICK-YOUR-OWN FARMS

36/6 SPRING GARDENS NURSERIES
Washington, West Sussex RH20 3BR
01903 – 892 225

36/7 ROCK FARM
The Hollow,
Washington, West Sussex RH20 3DB
01903 – 892 412

Paul Temple

Road Atlas for Gardeners

WASHINGTON – HENFIELD 36

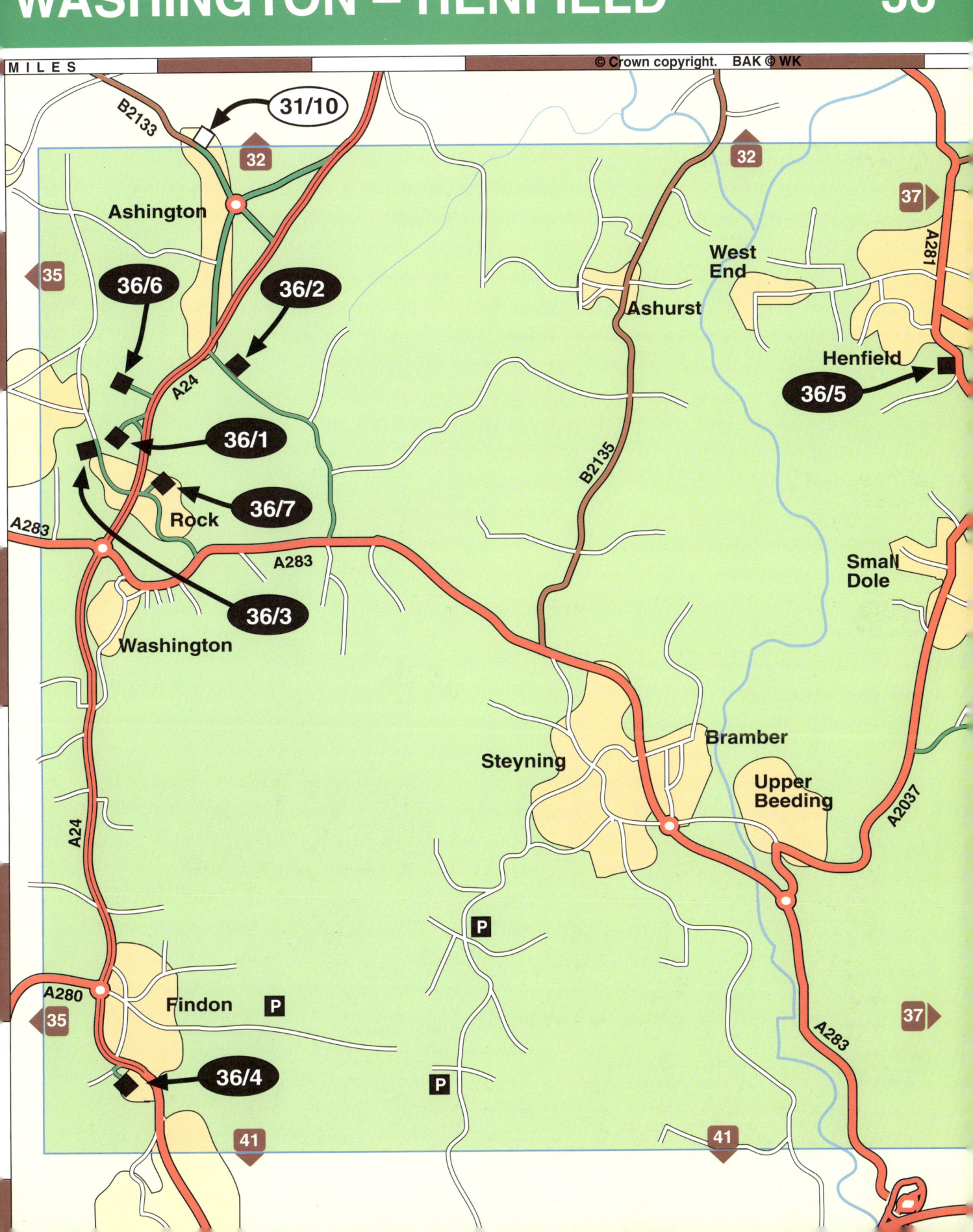

WEST SUSSEX

PICK-YOUR-OWN FARMS

37/1 **SWAINS FARM**
Henfield, West Sussex
01273 – 494 582

37/2 **ALBOURNE FARM PYO**
Albourne,
Hassocks, West Sussex, BN6 9DY
01273 – 833 683

NURSERIES & GARDEN CENTRES

37/3 **W. RUSSELL & SON LTD.**
Stonepound Nursery, Brighton Road,
Hassocks, West Sussex, BN6 9LZ
01273 – 843 754

37/4 **KINGS GARDEN CENTRE**
Brighton Road,
Hassocks, West Sussex, BN6 9LY
01273 – 845 232

37/5 **RUSHFIELDS PLANT CENTRE**
Henfield Road,
Poynings,
Near Brighton,
West Sussex
BN45 7AY
01273 – 857 445

All your plant needs are grown at Rushfields. Enjoy home-made cakes and speciality teas in the coffee shop.
Open: All year except Christmas – New Year.
Summer: 7 days a week 9 – 5.30.   Winter: Mondays – Fridays 9 – 4.30, Saturdays and Sundays 10 – 4.30.
Wheelchairs: Easy paved access.
Toilets: Yes.   **Dogs:** On lead.   **Credit cards:** Yes.

37/6 **HILLBROOK NURSERY**
Clappers Lane, Fulking,
Near Henfield, West Sussex BN5 9NH
01273 – 857 200

Paul Temple

Road Atlas for Gardeners

HENFIELD – HASSOCKS

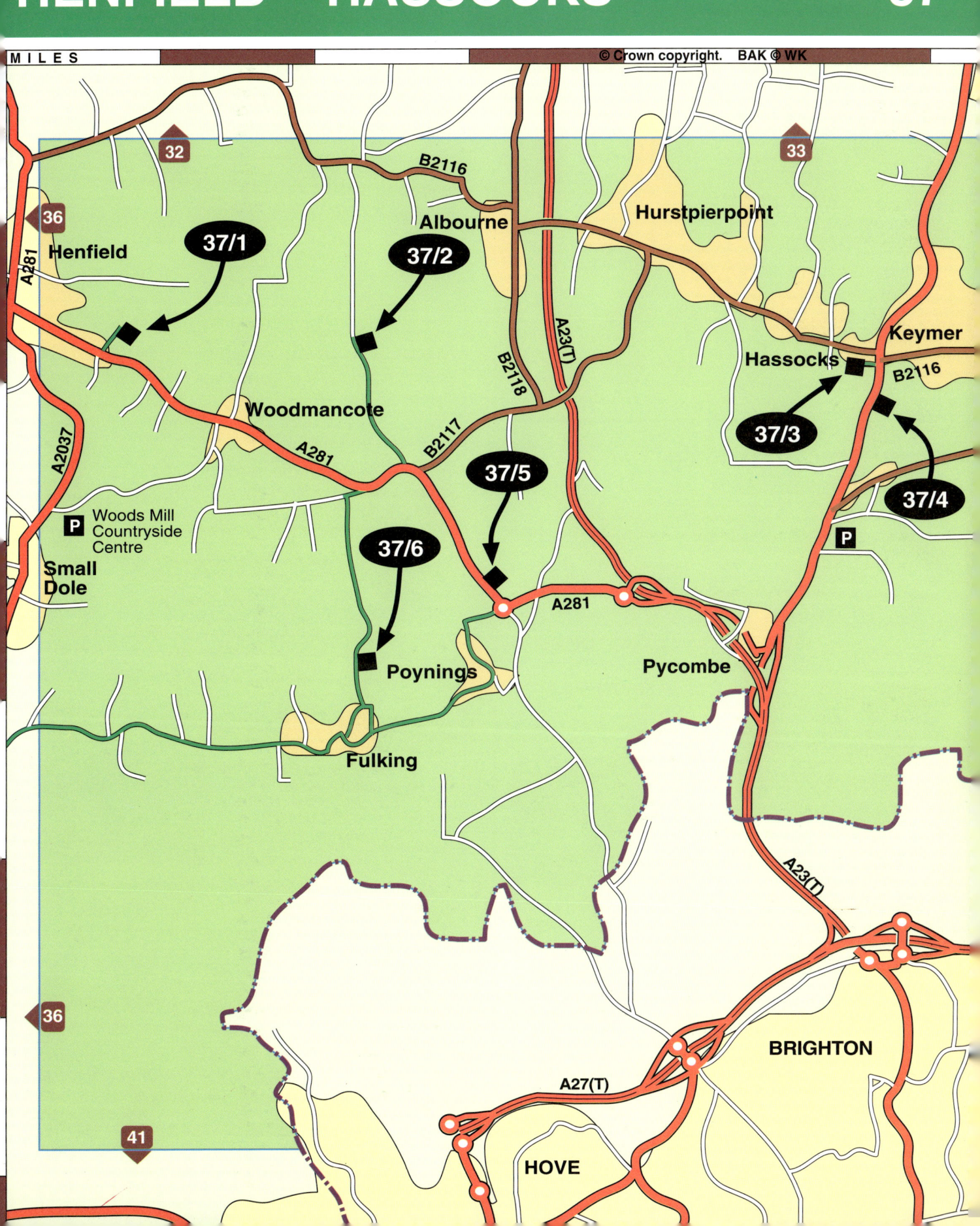

37

WEST SUSSEX

NURSERIES & GARDEN CENTRES

38/1 GREENACRE NURSERY
Main Road (A259), Chidham,
Near Chichester, West Sussex PO18 8TP
01243 – 572 441

A nursery specialising in spring and autumn bedding fuschias, geraniums, pansies, polys & hanging baskets.
Open: All year except Christmas and Boxing Days. 7 days a week, 9.30 – 5.30.
Wheelchairs: The whole area, including car park, is concreted.
Toilets: Ask if desperate.   **Dogs:** No.
Credit cards: American Express only.

38/2 BOSHAM BONSAI
Ratham Lane,
Bosham, West Sussex PO18 8NH
01243 – 573 388

38/3 BRINKMANS GARDEN CENTRE
Main Road,
Bosham, West Sussex, PO29 8QD
01243 – 573 696

38/4 BRAMBER NURSERY
Chichester Road,
West Wittering,
West Sussex
PO20 8QA
01243 – 512 004

Specialist nursery. Over 2000 varieties of trees and shrubs incl. over 250 varieties of roses. Garden furniture.
Open: All year except Christmas – New Year. 7 days a week. Winter: Mondays – Saturdays 8.30 – 4.30, Sundays 9.30 – 4.30. Summer: Mondays – Saturdays 8.30 – 5.30, Sundays 9.30 – 5.30.
Wheelchairs: Gravel car park, concrete inside.
Toilets: No.   **Dogs:** No.   **Credit cards:** Yes.

38/5 RUSSELL'S GARDEN CENTRE
Birdham,
Chichester, West Sussex PO20 7BV
01243 – 512 525

38/6 BELLFIELD NURSERY
Bell Lane,
Birdham,
Near Chichester,
West Sussex
PO20 7HY
01243 – 512 333

Family nursery growing geraniums, bedding plants, perennials, fuschias, hanging plants at very reasonable prices.
Open: All year except Christmas and Boxing Days; 6 days a week (CLOSED TUESDAYS); winter 8 – 5.30, summer 8 – 6.30.
Wheelchairs: Outside areas only.
Toilets: No.   **Dogs:** No.   **Credit cards:** No.

38/7 TAWNY NURSERIES
Bell Lane, Birdham,
Chichester, West Sussex PO20 7HV
01243 – 512 168

38/8 BEAVER NURSERY
Bell Lane,
Birdham,
Chichester,
West Sussex
PO20 7HY
01243 – 513 955

A nursery specialising in bedding and trailing plants, and hanging baskets. Dried flower arrangements.
Open: All year except Christmas, Boxing and New Year's Days. 7 days a week, 9 – 5.30.
Wheelchairs: Gravel car park.
Toilets: No.   **Dogs:** On lead.   **Credit cards:** Yes.

38/9 THE CUCKOO'S NEST NURSERY
125 Third Avenue, Almodington,
Near Chichester, West Sussex, PO20 7LB
01243 – 512 541

SOUTH WEST OF CHICHESTER 38

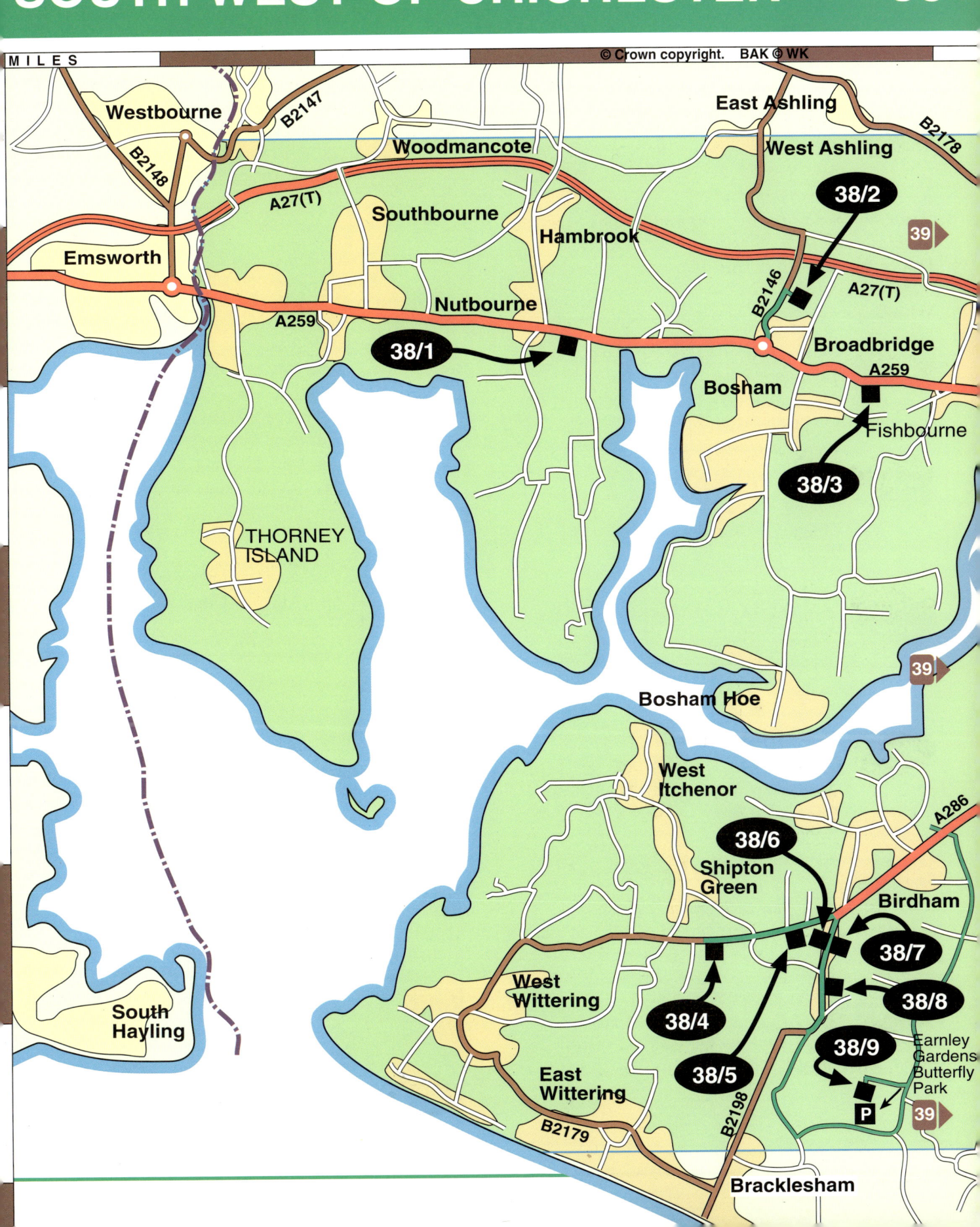

WEST SUSSEX

NURSERIES & GARDEN CENTRES

39/1 MAUDLIN NURSERY
Westhampnett,
Chichester, West Sussex PO18 0PB
01243 – 773 024

39/2 HOMEBASE

39/3 SHOPWHYKE NURSERIES
Tangmere Road, Shopwhyke,
Chichester, West Sussex PO20 6BL
01243 – 283 123

39/4 BRICK KILN NURSERY
Bognor Road,
Chichester, West Sussex PO20 6EJ
01243 – 531 700

39/5 COUNTRY GARDEN CENTRE
Bognor Road,
Chichester, West Sussex PO20 6EC
01243 – 789 276

39/6 APULDRAM ROSES
Apuldram Lane, Dell Quay,
Chichester, West Sussex PO20 7EE
01243 – 785 769

39/7 THE APULDRAM CENTRE
Common Farm, Apuldram Lane South,
Chichester, West Sussex PO20 7PF
01243 – 783 370

39/8 MANOR NURSERY
Lower Pagham Road, Runcton,
Chichester, West Sussex PO20 6LJ
01243 – 781 734

39/9 WOPHAMS LANE NURSERY
Wophams Lane,
Birdham, West Sussex PO20 7BR
01243 – 512 862

39/10 CHALCROFT NURSERIES AND GARDEN CENTRE
Chalcraft Lane,
Bognor Regis, West Sussex PO21 5TS
01243 – 863 346
Home-grown shrubs, conifers, herbaceous & bedding plants, ornamental & fruit trees. Garden supplies. Free advice.
Open: All year except Christmas, Boxing and New Year's Days. 7 days a week. Summer: Mondays – Saturdays 9 – 5.30, Sundays 9 – 5. Winter (when clocks change): Mondays – Saturdays 9 – 5, Sundays 9 – 4.
Wheelchairs: Flat paved and gravel areas.
Toilets: Ask if desperate.   **Dogs:** No.
Credit cards: Yes.

PICK-YOUR-OWN FARM

39/11 RUNCTON FARM
Pagham Road, Runcton,
Chichester, West Sussex PO20 6LJ
01243 – 787 849 (answerphone for PYO)

Road Atlas for Gardeners

CHICHESTER – BOGNOR REGIS 39

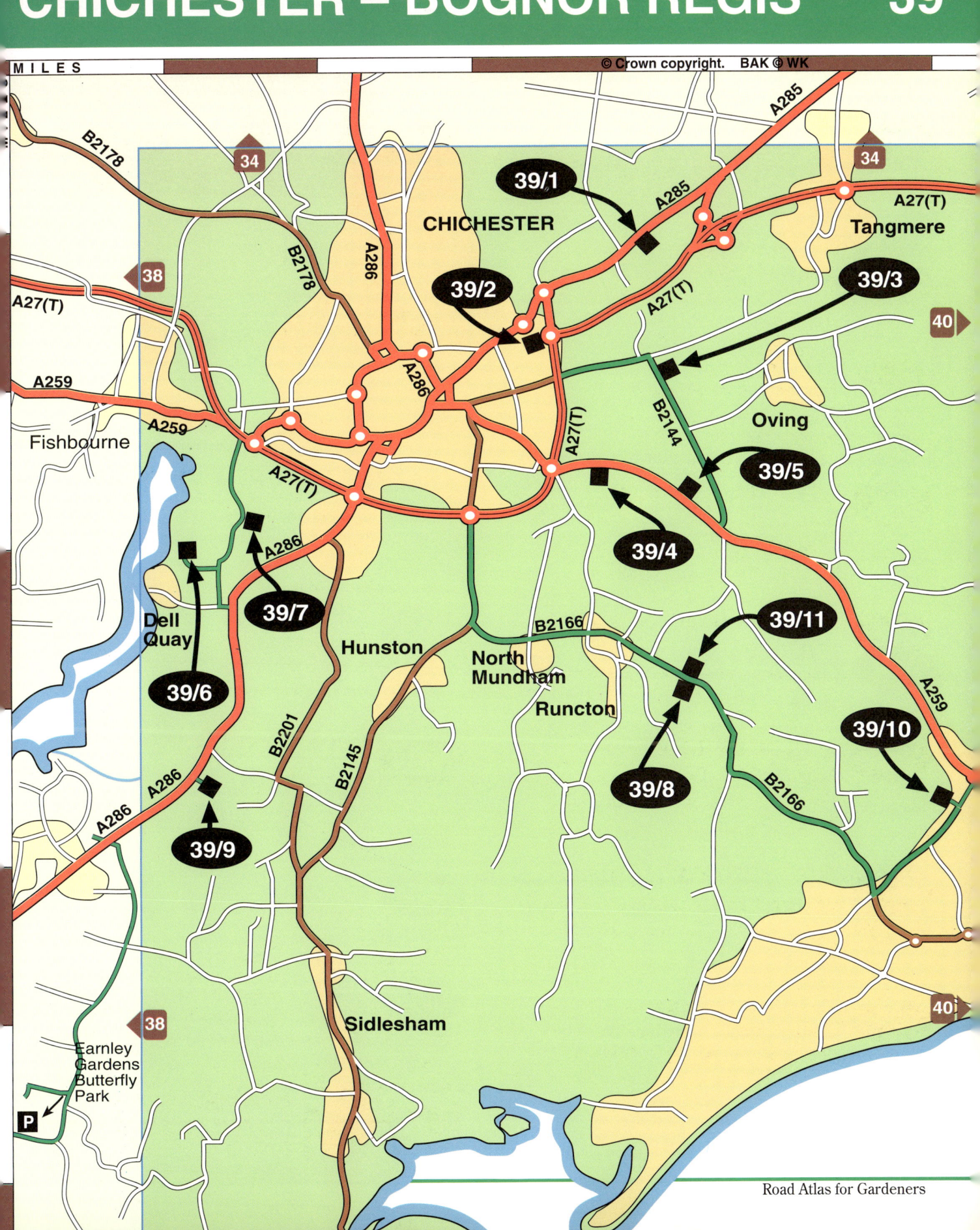

Road Atlas for Gardeners

WEST SUSSEX

NURSERIES & GARDEN CENTRES

40/1 ALDINGBOURNE COUNTRY CENTRE
Blackmill Lane, Norton,
Chichester, West Sussex PO18 0JR
01243 – 542 075

40/2 BASKET WORLD
Levelmere Lane, Eastergate,
Chichester, West Sussex PO20 6SA
01243 – 545 121

Specialist hanging basket and plant centre. Bedding plants, fuchsias and geraniums. Drinks.
Open: Mid-February – mid-November; 7 days a week, 9 – 5.
Wheelchairs: Flat concrete surfaces.
Toilets: Yes.   **Dogs:** No.   **Credit cards:** Yes.

SEE PAGE 42 FOR FULL DETAILS

40/3 NORTHFIELDS FARMHOUSE (COTTAGE PLANTS)
Open: March – October, FRIDAYS AND SUNDAYS ONLY, 10 – 5.

40/4 T. H. BECK & SON
Highfield & Sunnyside Nurseries,
Yapton Road, Barnham,
Bognor Regis, West Sussex PO22 0AX
01243 – 553 062

40/5 THE FLOWER BARN
37 Hill Lane,
Barnham, West Sussex PO22 0BL
01243 – 563 490

40/6 CROFTWAY NURSERY
Yapton Road, Barnham,
Bognor Regis, West Sussex PO22 0BH
01243 – 552 121

Growers of hardy perennials. Specialities incl. hardy geraniums & irises. Iris fields open May/June.
Open: February – November (CLOSED DECEMBER AND JANUARY); 7 days a week 9 – 5.30.
Wheelchairs: There are level gravel paths.
Toilets: Yes.   **Dogs:** On lead.   **Credit cards:** Yes.

40/7 MAPLETREES NURSERY
25 Yapton Road,
Bognor Regis,
West Sussex
PO22 0BQ
01243 – 552 028

Large old-established family nursery with all stock grown on the premises. Specialists in hanging baskets.
Open: All year except Christmas Day. 7 days a week. Mondays – Saturdays 8 – 5, Sundays 9 – 5.
Wheelchairs: Paved access.
Toilets: Yes.   **Dogs:** Yes.   **Credit cards:** Yes.

40/8 CINDERS LANE NURSERY
Bilsham Road,
Yapton, West Sussex BN18 0JJ
01243 – 552 555

40/9 THE COTTAGE NURSERY
Shripney Road,
Bognor Regis, West Sussex PO22 9PB
01243 – 860 324

40/10 ROOKERY FARM AND GARDEN CENTRE
Little Rookery, Hoe Lane, Flansham,
Bognor Regis, West Sussex PO22 8NM
01243 – 585 011

40/11 B & Q

GARDEN & GARDEN CENTRE

40/12 DENMANS GARDEN
Fontwell,
Near Arundel, West Sussex BN18 0SU
01243 – 542 808

Costs: Adults, £2.50; children, £1.50; senior citizens, £2.25.

Road Atlas for Gardeners

NORTH OF BOGNOR REGIS 40

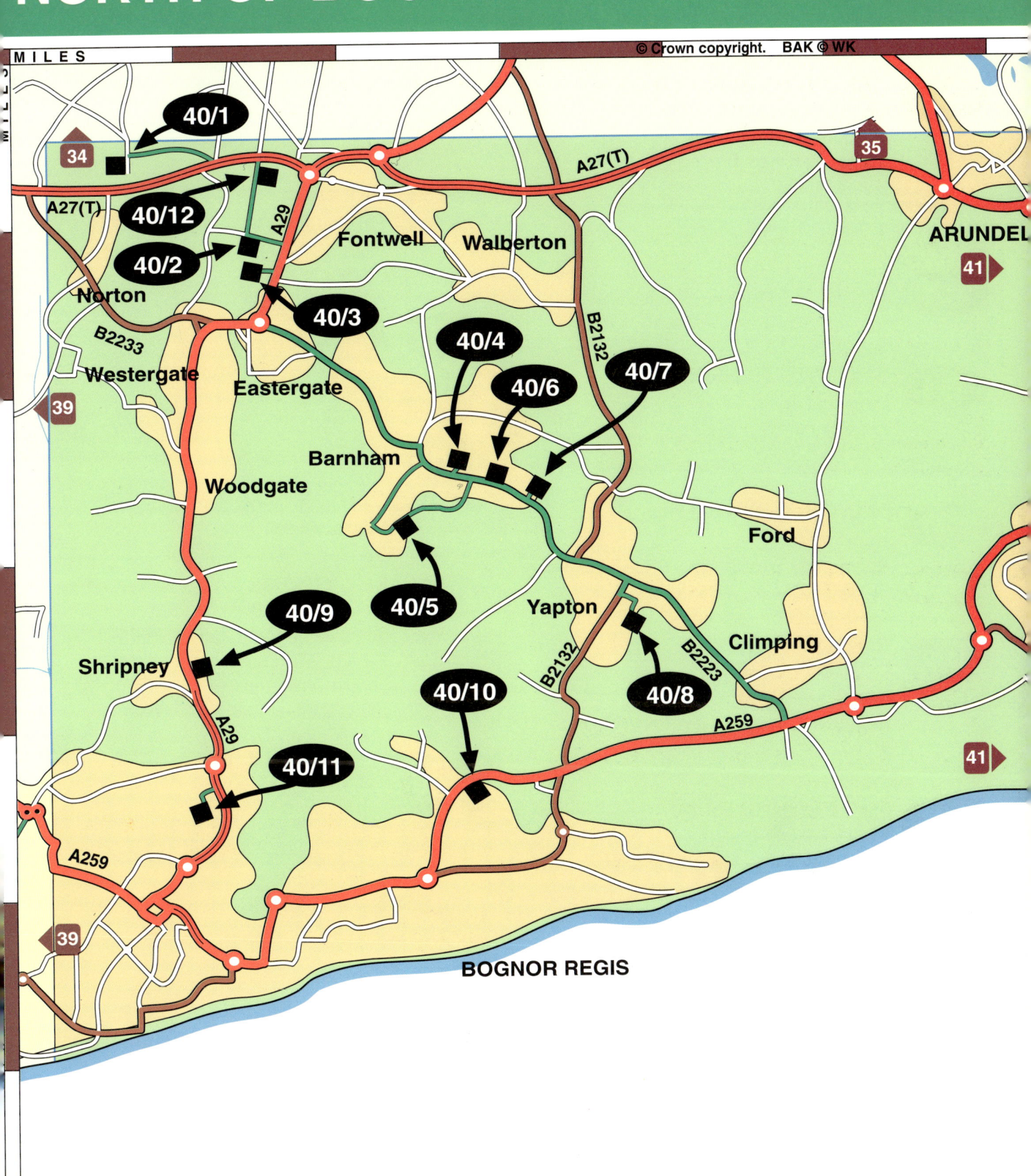

© Crown copyright. BAK © WK

Road Atlas for Gardeners

WEST SUSSEX

VINEYARD

41/1 ARUNDEL VINEYARDS
Church Lane,
Lyminster, West Sussex BN17 7QE
01903 – 883 393

NURSERIES & GARDEN CENTRES

41/2 FAIRHAVEN NURSERY

41/3 ST DENYS NURSERY
Dappers Lane,
Angmering, West Sussex
01903 – 773 240

41/4 MANOR NURSERIES
High Street,
Angmering, West Sussex BN16 4AV
01903 – 786 977

41/5 ROUNDSTONE GARDEN CENTRE
Roundstone By-pass,
Angmering, West Sussex BN16 4RD
01903 – 776 481/2/3

41/6 LOWERTREES NURSERY
Roundstone By-pass,
Angmering, West Sussex BN16 4BD
01903 – 770 457

41/7 WORTHING GARDEN CENTRE
Littlehampton Road, Ferring,
Worthing, West Sussex BN12 6PC
01903 – 242 003

41/8 GREENGOLD TREE FARM
Littlehampton Road,
Ferring, West Sussex BN12 6PC
01903 – 507 453

41/9 COUNTRY FAYRE
Littlehampton Road,
Ferring, West Sussex BN12 6PM
01903 – 245 123

41/10 FERRING NURSERIES
Littlehampton Road,
Ferring, West Sussex BN12 6PM
01903 – 784 569

41/11 B & Q

41/12 TEXAS GARDEN STORE

41/13 B & Q

PICK-YOUR-OWN FARM

41/14 ROUNDSTONE FARM SHOP & PICK-YOUR-OWN
Roundstone Farm, Littlehampton Road,
Ferring, West Sussex BN12 6PW
Shop 01903 – 783 817
PYO 01903 – 770 670/501 663

Plenty of free car parking. Tractor rides to each PYO crop. Large picnic area, drinks and ice-creams.
Open: Shop: all year, 7 days a week, Mondays – Saturdays 9 – 5, Sundays 10 – 4.
PYO: June – October, 7 days a week, 9 – 5.
Toilets: Yes.   **Dogs:** No.   **Credit cards:** No.

SEE PAGE 44 FOR FULL DETAILS

GARDEN

41/15 HIGHDOWN GARDENS

Open: 1 October – 31 March: Monday – Friday 10 – 4 (CLOSED WEEKENDS).   1 April – 30 September. Monday – Friday 10 – 6, Saturdays, Sundays & Bank Holidays 10 – 8.
Costs: Free.

Road Atlas for Gardeners

LITTLEHAMPTON – WORTHING 41

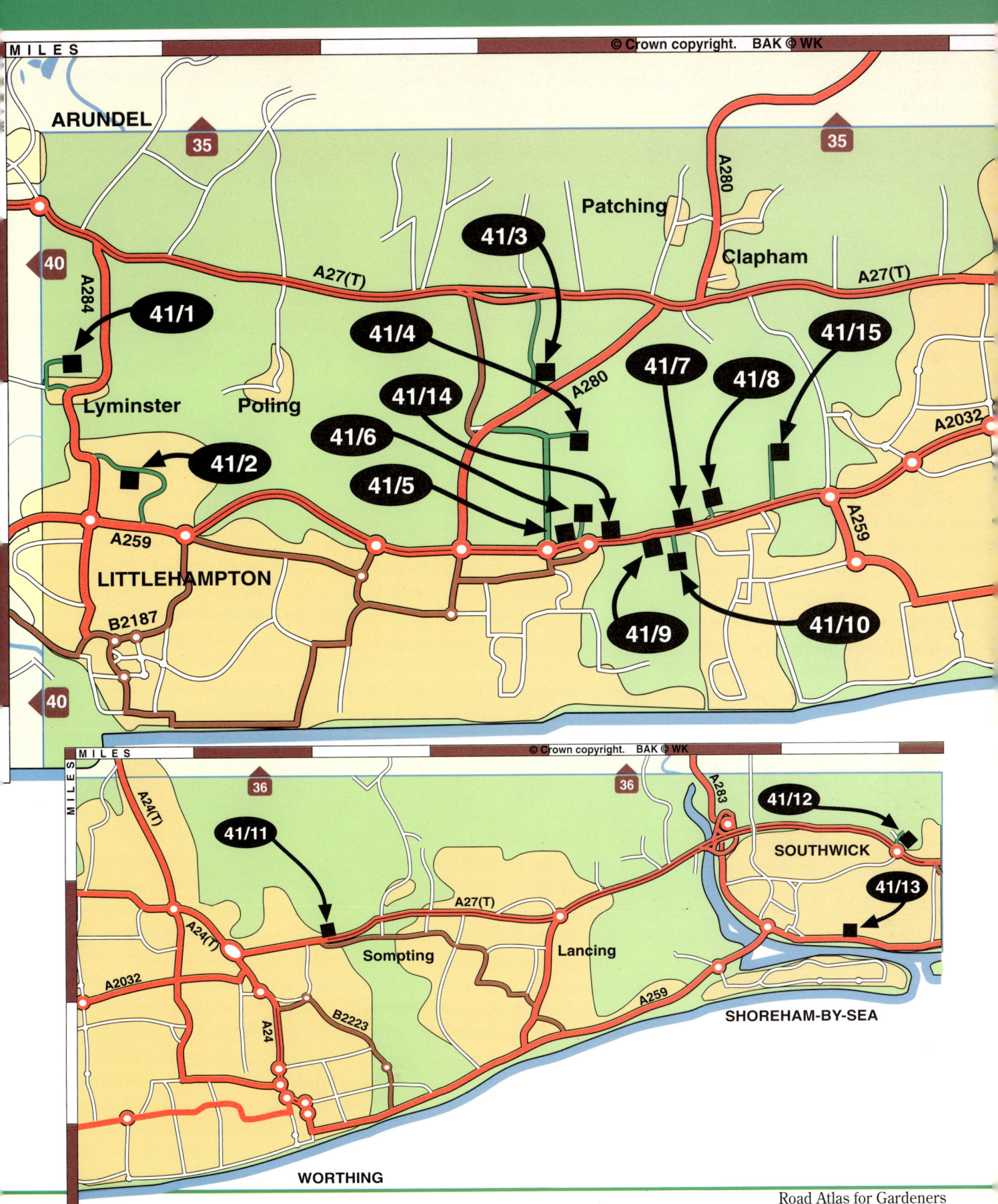

ADDITIONAL INFORMATION

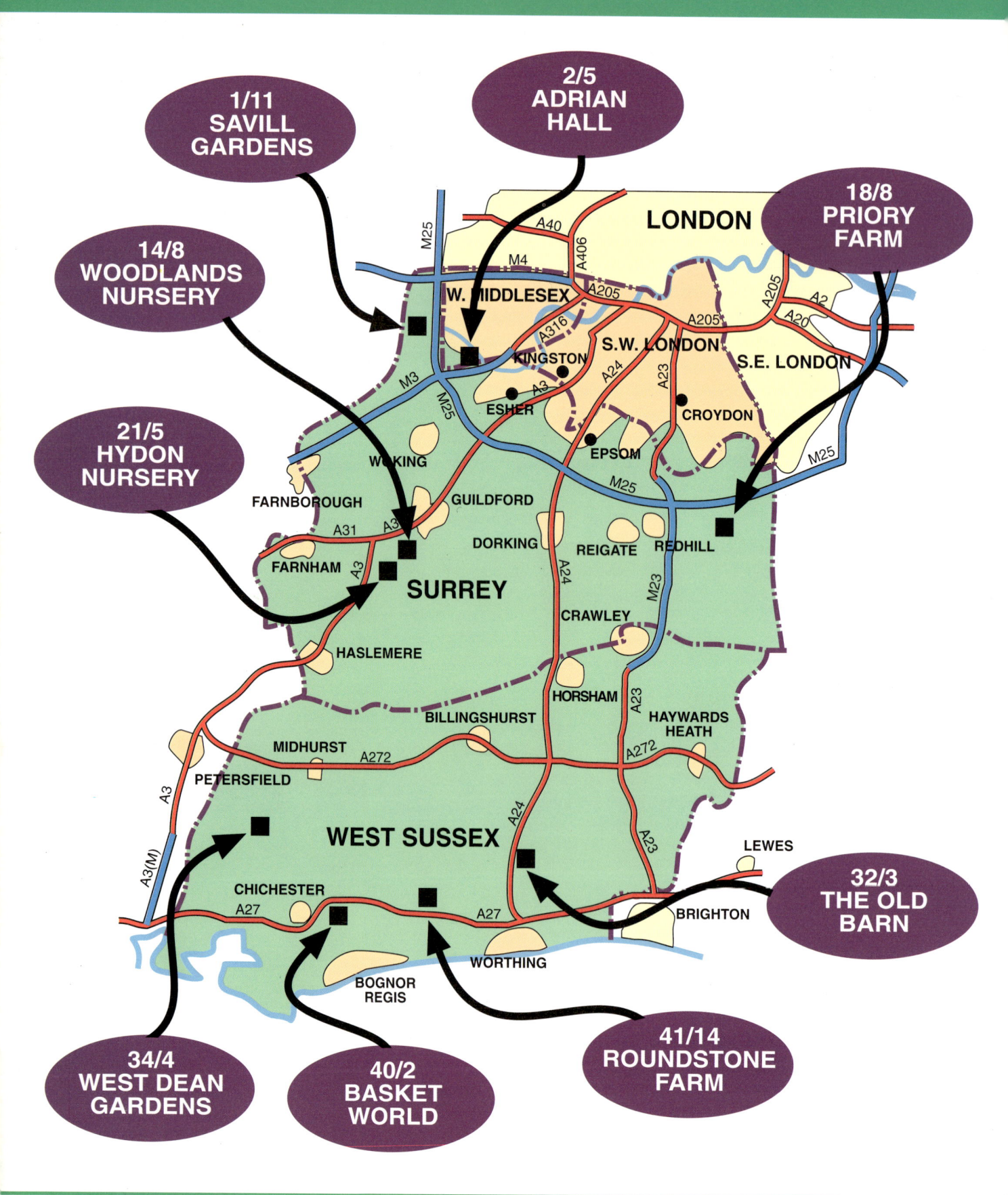

- 1/11 SAVILL GARDENS
- 2/5 ADRIAN HALL
- 18/8 PRIORY FARM
- 14/8 WOODLANDS NURSERY
- 21/5 HYDON NURSERY
- 32/3 THE OLD BARN
- 34/4 WEST DEAN GARDENS
- 40/2 BASKET WORLD
- 41/14 ROUNDSTONE FARM

Road Atlas for Gardeners

Basket World

SPECIALIST BASKET & PLANT CENTRE

Fontwell Park Nurseries Ltd

Levelmere Lane
Eastergate
Chichester
West-Sussex PO20 6SA
Tel (01243) 545 121

**Open mid February – mid November
7 days a week, 9–5**

Credit cards welcome, ample parking, toilets. No dogs please.
Flat concrete surfaces for wheelchairs: Disabled parking signs.
Tea and coffee machine.

2/5 "For all your garden needs"

Established over 30 years

A full and unique selection of plants and garden requisites for every season. Specialist suppliers of garden construction materials, with display garden showing over 50 different paving styles. – Also planting containers, statuary and water features.

Adrian Hall LTD

ADRIAN HALL LTD
THE GARDEN CENTRE
FELTHAM HILL ROAD, FELTHAM, MIDDX
(0181) 890 5057

18/8 PRIORY FARM

NUTFIELD   REDHILL   SURREY
A GARDENER'S DAY OUT

Plant Centre: Enjoy the wide range of exceptional quality bedding, pot and perennial plants available throughout spring, summer and autumn.

Farm Shop: Enjoy our up market country food shop situated in the restored Victorian stone-built farm buildings. There are many mouth-watering products and interesting gifts.

Pick-Your-Own: Enjoy our parkland setting with large car parks, lakes and many crops including asparagus, raspberries, strawberries and cherries.

Coffee Shop: Enjoy a relaxing cup of tea with home made cakes or have a light lunch in picturesque surroundings.

OPEN EVERY DAY
9am to 5pm
Summer extension to 6pm during June, July, August

Plant Centre closed Jan, Feb
Coffee Shop closed Jan, Feb, March

Tel: (01737) 823 304

14/8 ROBERT GRIMMOND

**THE GREEN
WOOD STREET VILLAGE,
NR. GUILDFORD**

ANTIQUE & SECONDHAND GARDEN ORNAMENTS & RECLAIMED MATERIALS
MATURE CONIFERS, TREES, SHRUBS & HEDGING
CHRISTMAS TREES

GATES
STONE SINKS & TROUGHS
STATUARY
COBBLESTONES
WALLING STONE
CHIMNEY POTS
RAILWAY SLEEPERS
VICTORIAN EDGINGS
YORK FLAGS, BRICKS
MUSHROOM STONES
PAVIORS & SETTS
BALUSTRADING
URNS & POTS
LAMP POSTS
BOUGHT & SOLD
APPOINTMENT ONLY

Woodlands Farm Nursery

(01483) 235536

MOBILE **(0374) 741321**

32/3 OLD BARN NURSERIES

*Retail Nursery & Old Barn Pantry
Run by Growers for Gardeners*

Open: 9–6 Monday-Saturday; 10.30–4.30 Sunday
Old Barn Pantry open 9–6 every day

★★★★
Visit our glorious centre for top quality and exceptional value.
★★★★

Special seasonal displays from home grown bedding plants & wide range of roses in spring to wonderful Christmas displays from early October.

★★★★

Excellent silk and dried flowers.
An Aladdin's cave of gift ideas.
Relax and enjoy our home made cakes & hot daily specials served till 5pm.
Enjoy breakfast, coffee, lunch or tea in 'The Old Barn Pantry'
FOR QUALITY, FOR CHOICE, FOR YOU
All major credit cards accepted
OLD BARN NURSERIES, DIAL POST (A24)
Telephone: (01403) 710 000

Hydon Nurseries

21/5

Specialist growers of Rhododendrons, Azaleas, Camellias & Magnolias.

Large selection of newer and more unusual hybrids including the smaller garden Yakushimanum varieties.

LARGE SPECIMEN PLANTS AVAILABLE LIST ON APPLICATION

Nursery open 8am to 5pm Monday to Saturday.
(lunch-time closing 12.45 to 2pm) Visitors welcome.

COLOUR ILLUSTRATED CATALOGUE £1.50

Clock Barn Lane,
Hydon Heath, Godalming,
Surrey GU8 4AZ
(close to the West Surrey Cheshire Home)
Tel: 01483 860252
Fax: 01483 419937

The Edwardian Country Garden at West Dean

34/4

35 acre South Downs garden in a tranquil valley setting with herbaceous borders, 300' pergola, water gardens and magnificent trees. Ideal for an afternoon's relaxation. Savour the Edwardian atmosphere of the newly restored 2.5 acre Walled Kitchen Garden, bursting with fruit, vegetables and flowers. Wander through the 13 historic glasshouses scented with carnations, melons, figs and many other exotic plants, or stroll the 2.25 mile Parkland Walk to the crest of the downs and the 45 acre St. Roches Arboretum with its splendid trees and shrubs.

New 'Prince of Wales Institute of Architecture' designed Visitor Centre, open Spring 1995.

**Licensed Restaurant
Shop & Plant Centre**
Excellent facilities for coach parties

**Open daily 11.00am–5.00pm
April to October inclusive**

Parties must be pre-booked, telephone 01243 811303

West Dean Gardens,
near Chichester,
West Sussex PO18 0QZ

The first atlas in the series!

Road Atlas for Gardeners

Nearly 200 places for gardeners to visit in

Derbyshire, Nottinghamshire & S. Yorkshire

"An unusual and valuable book"
Dr. Brent Elliott,
Librarian, Royal Horticultural Society,
"The Bookseller"

Available locally at £6.95 from W. H. Smith, Bookshops and Garden Centres

Stockists include Floralands, Lambley: Brookfields, Nottingham; Reuben Shaw, Newthorpe; Sandhurst Nurseries, Walesby; Bardills, Stapleford; Cannon Hall, Barnsley; Greenwood Bonsai, Arnold; The Dukeries, Welbeck

Or direct from the publishers,
The Factory Shop Guide,
1 Rosebery Mews, Rosebery Road, London, SW2 4DQ, (£6.95 + £1.00 p&p)
Order with a credit card now by phoning
0181 – 678 0593

The Savill Garden

1/11

Enjoy the peace, beauty and tranquillity of this outstanding 35 acre woodland garden

in Windsor Great Park

Spring brings a wealth of daffodils, rhododendrons, azaleas, camellias, magnolias and much more.
Summer features the extensive rose gardens, herbaceous borders and alpine plantings.
Autumn offers a breath-taking array of foliage colour and fruit.
Winter is far from dull, particularly for the discerning gardener.

**NEW TEMPERATE HOUSE
OPEN SPRING 1995**

OPEN DAILY: 10am–6pm Mar–Oct; 10am–4pm Nov–Feb
Licensed Restaurant • Gift Shop • Plant Centre
Admission: Adults £3.30; Senior Citizens £2.80; Parties 20+ £2.80
Accompanied Children free

A GARDEN FOR ALL SEASONS

*Situated in Wick Lane, Englefield Green, Surrey (off A30)
Signposted from Ascot, Egham (M25) & Windsor (M4)*

Free car/coach parking

Enquiries: (01753) 860222

Check our CROP CALENDAR

	JUNE	JULY	AUG	SEPT
Strawberries		✓	✓	✓
Raspberries		✓		
Autumn Bliss Raspberries			✓	✓
Loganberries		✓	✓	
Gooseberries	✓	✓		
Black Currants		✓	✓	
Red Currants		✓	✓	
Victoria Plums			✓	✓
Dessert & Cooking Apples			✓	✓
Rhubarb	✓	✓		
Cabbage	✓	✓	✓	✓
Calabrese	✓	✓	✓	✓
Cauliflowers			✓	✓
Courgettes			✓	✓
Peas	✓	✓		
Mange Tout	✓	✓		
Broad Beans	✓	✓		
French Beans			✓	✓
Runner Beans			✓	✓
Carrots		✓	✓	✓
Onions			✓	✓
Beetroot		✓	✓	✓
Spinach		✓	✓	✓
Marrows		✓	✓	✓
Pumpkins				
Sweetcorn			✓	✓
Super Sweet Corn			✓	✓
Wallflower Plants				✓
Potatoes for Winter Storage *(Farm Shop)*				✓

Pick-Your-Own is open:
7 days a week
9.00 – 5.00
from June – Oct

Want to know what's ready for picking?
Call our 24-hour Crop-Line on (01903) 770670 or 501663

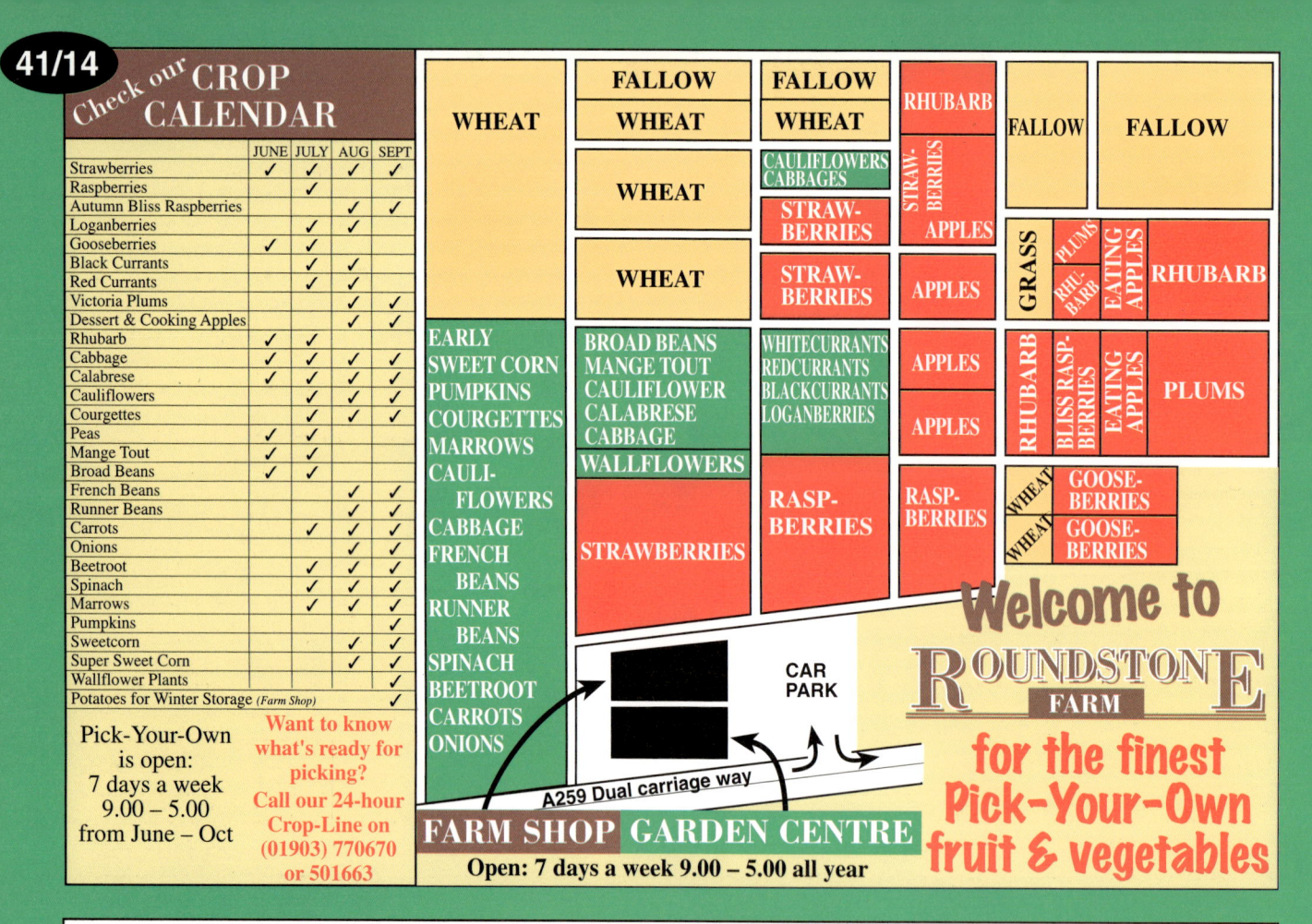

Welcome to ROUNDSTONE FARM
for the finest Pick-Your-Own fruit & vegetables

FARM SHOP   GARDEN CENTRE
Open: 7 days a week 9.00 – 5.00 all year

A259 Dual carriage way

Perfect companions for your days out!

This unique series of books – essential reading for locals and visitors alike – pinpoints which companies have their own shops selling terrific value perfects, seconds, ends of lines and slightly substandard goods direct to the public at greatly reduced prices. Specially drawn maps and personally researched detailed descriptions lead you straight to these elusive shops.

Buy direct from manufacturers in the South-East.

The Factory Shop Guides are the only books published in Britain which give you the low-down on how, when and where to save money by buying direct from the manufacturer. Opening times, holiday dates, parking, factory tours, access for disabled people and parents with prams, and credit card details are listed – even where to find teashops and toilets so that all the family can browse in comfort. All you need for a great day out!

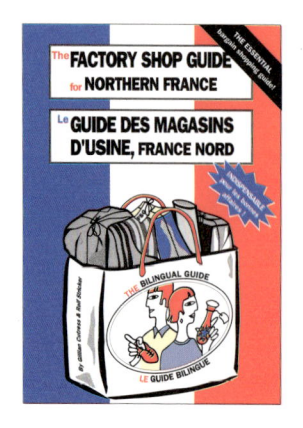

Discover French factory shop secrets from Calais southwards.

From good bookshops or directly from the publisher: The Factory Shop Guide, 1 Rosebery Mews, Rosebery Road, London SW2 4DQ. Or phone for details or order by credit card on (0181) 678 0593.

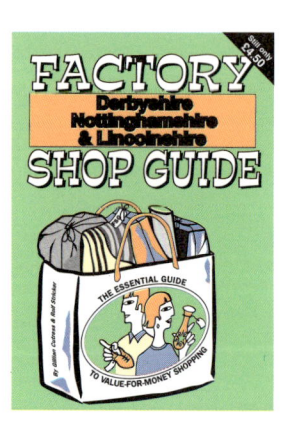

Combine gardens and shopping around the Peak district.

INDEX

NURSERIES, PLANT & GARDEN CENTRES

ACE NURSERY	31/6
ADRIAN HALL, Feltham	2/5 & page 43
ADRIAN HALL, Putney	4/4
ALDINGBOURNE COUNTRY CENTRE	40/1
ALFOLD GARDEN CENTRE	25/1
APULDRAM CENTRE, THE	39/7
APULDRAM ROSES	39/6
ARCHITECTURAL PLANTS	32/1
ASTOLAT	21/3
AYLINGS OF TROTTON	29/2
B & Q, Bognor Regis	40/11
B & Q, Crawley	27/2
B & Q, Croydon	13/3
B & Q, Guildford	15/5
B & Q, Leatherhead	16/1
B & Q, New Malden	10/2
B & Q, Shoreham	41/13
B & Q, Surbiton	10/3
B & Q, Wandsworth	5/1
B & Q, Wimbledon	4/6
B & Q, Worthing	41/11
BADSHOT LEA GARDEN CENTRE	19/2
BARNES NURSERY	12/6
BARRALETS NURSERY	14/6
BARROW HILL NURSERY	36/5
BASKET WORLD	40/2 & page 42
BEADLE, G.J.	12/5
BEAVER NURSERY	38/8
BECK, T.H. & SON	40/4
BEECHCROFT NURSERY	11/4
BELLFIELD NURSERY	38/6
BLACKGATE LANE NURSERY	31/1
BLACKHORSE PLANTS	14/3
BOLNEY NURSERY	33/3
BOSHAM BONSAI	38/2
BOURNE HILL NURSERY	26/2
BOURNE MILL GARDEN CENTRE	19/4
BOURNE VALLEY GARDEN CENTRE	8/9
BRAMBER NURSERY	38/4
BRIAN HILEY	12/4
BRIARWOOD NURSERY	15/1
BRICK KILN NURSERY	39/4
BRINKMANS GARDEN CENTRE	38/3
BROOK NURSERY	6/8
BROOK NURSERY & PLANT CENTRE	24/2
BRYAN'S GARDEN CENTRE	5/4
BUCKLAND NURSERIES	17/4
CBF NURSERIES	32/2
CEDAR NURSERY	16/2
CHALCROFT NURSERIES	39/10
CHEALS GARDEN CENTRE	27/3
CHESSINGTON GARDEN CENTRE	9/5
CHOBHAM NURSERIES	7/3
CINDERS LANE NURSERY	40/8
CLANDON PARK GARDEN CENTRE	15/11
CLARKE, S.G.	11/7
CLAY LANE NURSERY	18/4
COBHAM PARK NURSERY	9/6
COMPTON NURSERY	20/2
COOMBE WOOD GARDENS & NURSERY	13/11
COOMBLAND GARDENS	31/7
COPPED HALL COTTAGE GARDENS	6/7
COTTAGE NURSERY, THE	40/9
COULSDON GARDEN MARKET	13/7
COUNTRY FAYRE	41/9
COUNTRY GARDEN CENTRE, Chichester	39/5
COUNTRY GARDEN CENTRE, Dorking	17/3
COUNTRY GARDEN CENTRE, Windlesham	6/3
COUNTRY GARDENS AT HANDCROSS	33/1
CROCKFORD PARK GARDEN CENTRE	8/7
CROCKNORTH NURSERY	16/6
CROFTWAY NURSERY	40/6
CROYDON GARDEN CENTRE	13/5
CUCKOO'S NEST NURSERY, THE	38/9
DEMETRIADI, K	21/1
D.I.Y. GARDEN CENTRE	10/9
DENMANS GARDEN	40/12
DO IT ALL, Epsom	10/6
DOBBE, A. J. AND SONS	10/10
DOBBE'S NURSERIES	16/4
DOVES BARN NURSERY	23/4
EAST ASHLING NURSERIES	34/1
EGHAM GARDEN CENTRE	1/7
ELM NURSERY	15/3
FAIRHAVEN NURSERY	41/2
FANNY'S FARM SHOP	17/1
FARM LANE NURSERIES	10/8
FERRING NURSERIES	41/10
FLITTON'S NURSERY AND PLANT CENTRE	12/8
FLOWER BARN, THE	40/5
FRANK FAIRHEAD, Laleham	1/5
FRANK FAIRHEAD, Staines	1/4
FRENSHAM GARDEN CENTRE	19/5
GARDEN CARE SUPPLIES	10/4
GARDEN MARKET, THE	13/4
GARDEN STYLE	19/6
GARSON FARM	9/9
GLEN AND NURSERY, THE	14/9
GREAT MILLS, Twickenham	2/8
GREENACRE NURSERY	38/1
GREENGOLD TREE FARM	41/8
GREENWAYS NURSERY	31/4
GRINSTEAD NURSERIES	30/1
HAZELBANK NURSERY	20/3
HEATHFIELD NURSERIES	17/7
HEATH NURSERY (LEYLANDII)	21/2
HEATHROW GARDEN CENTRE	2/1
HERBS AND SCENTED PLANTS	16/7
HERONS BONSAI NURSERY	24/6
HIDDEN GARDEN, THE	8/3
HIGH BEECHES NURSERIES	27/5
HIGH TREES NURSERIES	17/5
HIGHBANKS NURSERY	21/4
HILL BROOK NURSERY	37/6
HILL PARK ROSES	9/2

Road Atlas for Gardeners

INDEX

HILLIER GARDEN CENTRE, Horsham	26/3
HILLIER GARDEN CENTRE, Windlesham	6/2
HILLSIDE SHRUBS & HARDY PLANTS NURSERY	23/2
HOLE STREET NURSERIES	36/2
HOLLY GATE CACTUS NURSERY	31/10
HOMEBASE, Camberley	6/6
HOMEBASE, Chichester	39/2
HOMEBASE, Crawley	27/1
HOMEBASE, Croydon	13/1
HOMEBASE, Guildford	15/6
HOMEBASE, Hampton	2/9
HOMEBASE, Isleworth	3/2
HOMEBASE, New Malden	4/5
HOMEBASE, Richmond	4/1
HOMEBASE, Walton-on-Thames	8/11
HOMEBASE, Wandsworth	5/2
HOMEBASE, Wimbledon	5/3
HOMEBASE, Woking	14/1
HOMELEIGH NURSERY	21/7
HOUNSLOW GARDEN CENTRE	2/6
HOWARDS NURSERY CENTRE	27/4
HYDON NURSERIES	21/5 & page 43
INGWERSEN, W.E.Th	28/3
IVY MILL NURSERY	18/5
JACKMAN'S GARDEN CENTRE	15/2
JACKSWOOD GARDEN CENTRE	36/4
JACKSWOOD GARDEN CENTRE	23/5
JACQUES CANN OF WEYBRIDGE	8/10
JOHN GUNNER GARDEN CENTRE	14/5
JOHN TRAIN PLANTS	1/2
JUNGLE GARDEN CENTRE	8/4
KENNEDYS GARDEN CENTRE, Claygate	9/4
KENNEDYS GARDEN CENTRE, Croydon	13/8
KINGS GARDEN CENTRE	37/4
KNAPHILL GARDEN CENTRE	7/6
KNIGHTS GARDEN CENTRE, Chelsham	18/2
KNIGHTS GARDEN CENTRE, Godstone	18/7
KNIGHTS GARDEN CENTRE, Woldingham	18/3
LAKESIDE GARDEN CENTRE	2/4
LALEHAM NURSERIES	8/1
LAURENCE HOBBS ORCHIDS	24/8
LAWMANS GARDEN CENTRE	13/2
LINCLUDEN NURSERY	6/9
LITTLE ACRES NURSERY	19/3
LONGACRES NURSERY	6/4
LOWER ROAD PLANT CENTRE	16/3
LOWERTREES NURSERY	41/6
LOXWOOD NURSERIES	25/2
MANOR NURSERIES	41/4
MANOR NURSERY	39/8
MAPLETREES NURSERY	40/7
MARSDEN NURSERY AND GARDEN CENTRE	10/7
MARYLANDS NURSERY	33/4
MAUDLIN NURSERY	39/1
MAYFLOWER NURSERIES	1/8
MELBOURNE NURSERY	12/2
MERRIST WOOD PLANT CENTRE	14/2
MICHAEL SEYMOUR NURSERY, THE	17/2
MILLAIS NURSERIES	19/7
MIMBRIDGE GARDEN CENTRE	7/5
MONKTON NURSERIES	19/1
MORDEN HALL GARDEN CENTRE	11/1
MURRELLS NURSERY	31/2
NETTLETON'S NURSERY	18/6
NEWBRIDGE NURSERIES	26/1
NORTHFIELDS FARMHOUSE (COTTAGE PLANTS)	40/3
NOTCUTTS GARDEN CENTRE, Cranleigh	21/6
NOTCUTTS GARDEN CENTRE, Laleham	1/6
NOTCUTTS WATERERS NURSERIES, Bagshot	6/5
NURSERY, THE	8/5
NURSERY COURT GARDENS	6/1
NUTFIELD NURSERIES	23/1
OAK LODGE NURSERIES	20/1
OCCASIONALLY YOURS	24/4
OLD BARN NURSERIES	32/3 & page 43
OLD GARDENS, THE	14/4
OLD NURSERY GARDEN, THE	36/3
ORCHARD NURSERY	24/9
OSTERLEY GARDEN CENTRE	3/1
OTTER NURSERY, THE	8/8
PALM CENTRE, THE	4/2
PANNELLS GARDEN CENTRE	2/3
PANTILES NURSERIES	7/1
PETERSHAM NURSERIES	3/3
PETERS PLANTS AND GARDEN CENTRE	9/8
PLANT CENTRE, THE	7/2
PLANTS 'N' GARDENS	28/2
PRIORY FARM	18/8 & page 43
PUMPKIN COTTAGE	34/2
REIGATE GARDEN CENTRE	17/8
RIPLEY NURSERIES	15/4
RIVERSIDE NURSERIES	7/4
RIVERVIEW GARDEN CENTRE	30/3
ROCKHAM NURSERY	11/5
ROCKINGHAMS GARDEN CENTRE	4/3
ROOKERY FARM & GARDEN CENTRE	40/10
ROTHERHILL NURSERIES & GARDEN CENTRE	29/1
ROUNDSTONE FARM SHOP & PYO	41/14 & page 44
ROUNDSTONE GARDEN CENTRE	41/5
RUSHFIELDS PLANT CENTRE	37/5
RUSKIN ROAD GARDEN CENTRE	12/1
RUSSELL, W. & SON	37/3
RUSSELL'S GARDEN CENTRE	38/5
SCAYNES HILL NURSERY	33/5
SECRETTS GARDEN CENTRE	20/6
SEYMOURS GARDEN & LEISURE CENTRE	10/5
SHOPWHYKE NURSERIES	39/3
SNOW HILL GARDEN CENTRE	23/3
SQUIRE'S GARDEN CENTRE, Twickenham	2/7
SQUIRE'S GARDEN CENTRE, Chertsey	8/12
SQUIRE'S GARDEN CENTRE, Hersham	9/1
SQUIRE'S GARDEN CENTRE, Shepperton	8/2
SQUIRES GARDEN CENTRE, Woking	7/7
ST DENYS NURSERY	41/3
STANBRIDGE VIEW NURSERY	33/2
SUTTON GREEN GARDEN NURSERY	15/7

Road Atlas for Gardeners